FOUNDATIONS OF DEMOCRACY IN THE EUROPEAN UNION

Foundations of Democracy in the European Union

From the Genesis of Parliamentary Democracy to the European Parliament

Edited by

John Pinder

Foreword by

HRH Princess Margriet of The Netherlands

 in association with
EUROPEAN CULTURAL FOUNDATION

First published in Great Britain 1999 by
MACMILLAN PRESS LTD
Houndmills, Basingstoke, Hampshire RG21 6XS and London
Companies and representatives throughout the world

A catalogue record for this book is available from the British Library.

ISBN 0–333–77470–1

 First published in the United States of America 1999 by
ST. MARTIN'S PRESS, INC.,
Scholarly and Reference Division,
175 Fifth Avenue, New York, N.Y. 10010

ISBN 0–312–22296–3

Library of Congress Cataloging-in-Publication Data
Foundations of democracy in the European Union : from the genesis of
parliamentary democracy to the European Parliament / edited by John
Pinder ; foreword by Princess Margriet of The Netherlands.
p. cm.
"In association with European Cultural Foundation-Fondation
Européenne de la Culture."
Papers from a conference held at St. George's House, Windsor
Castle, on 12–13 April, 1996.
Includes bibliographical references and index.
ISBN 0–312–22296–3 (cloth)
1. Democracy—Europe, Western—History—Congresses.   2. European
Parliament—Congresses.   I. Pinder, John.
JN94.A91F68   1999
321.8'094—DC21   98–55306
                                                                  CIP

This book is printed on paper suitable for recycling and made from fully managed and
sustained forest sources.

10   9   8   7   6   5   4   3   2   1
08   07   06   05   04   03   02   01   00   99

Printed and bound in Great Britain by
Antony Rowe Ltd, Chippenham, Wiltshire

Contents

Notes on Contributors

Colin Bonwick is Professor of American History at Keele University. His publications include *English Radicals and the American Revolution* and *The American Revolution.*

Richard Corbett is a Member of the European Parliament. He was formerly Deputy Secretary-General of the Socialist Group in the European Parliament. His publications include *The European Parliament* (with Francis Jacobs and Michael Shackleton) and *The European Parliament's Role in European Union Integration.*

Anthony Glees is Reader in Government at Brunel University. His publications include *Reinventing Germany: German Political Relations since 1945* and *Exile Politics During the Second World War: The German Social Democrats in Britain.*

Jonathan I. Israel has been Professor of Dutch History and Institutions at the University of London since 1985 and is a fellow of the British Academy and a foreign member of the Royal Netherlands Academy of Sciences. His books include *The Anglo-Dutch Moment* (editor and co-author), *Dutch Primacy in World Trade, 1585–1740* and *The Dutch Republic: Its Rise, Greatness and Fall, 1477–1806.*

E.H. Kossmann was Professor of Dutch History and Institutions at University College London 1957–66 and Professor of Modern History at the University of Groningen 1966–87. His books include *Texts Concerning the Revolt of the Netherlands* (with A.F. Mellink), *The Low Countries 1780–1940* and five volumes of *Britain and the Netherlands* (co-edited with J.S. Bromley).

John Pinder was Director of the Policy Studies Institute, 1964–85, and is Visiting Professor at the College of Europe, Bruges. His books include *The European Community and Eastern Europe*, *Federal Union: The Pioneers – A History of Federal Union* (with Richard Mayne) and *The Building of the European Union.*

R.C. Van Caenegem was appointed Professor at the University of Ghent in 1964 and is now Professor Emeritus. He was President of the Koninklijke

Academie voor Wetenschappen, Letteren en Schone Kunsten van België in 1988, was made a Baron in 1994 for his services to history and is a corresponding Fellow of the British Academy. His books include *The Birth of English Common Law*; *Judges, Legislators and Professors. Chapter in English Legal History* (Goodhart Lectures 1984–1985); and *An Historical Introduction to Western Constitutional Law*.

Bernard Voyenne was Professor at the Centre de formation et de perfectionnement des Journalistes, Paris, 1949–80. He was a journalist with *Ce Soir* and *Combat* and director of the *Revue de la penseé française*. His books include *Textes choisis de P.-J. Proudhon, Histoire de l'ideé européenne* and *Histoire de l'idée fédéraliste*, 3 vols.

Preface

This book is the product of a study whose initial aim was to assess the historic contribution of Britain and the Low Countries to the development of democracy in Europe up to the present time. Papers on this theme were discussed at a conference at St George's House, Windsor Castle, on 12–13 April 1996. The papers, on which the chapters of this book are based, were contributed by specialists on each of seven stages in the process. As the study proceeded, the broader significance of the theme emerged. The chapters not only show how much Britain gained from the pre-democratic developments in the Low Countries up to the time when William and Mary acceded to the English throne and how democracy in Europe has gained from the consequent success and spread of parliamentary government; they also demonstrate ways in which democratic principles and practice can be transferred across frontiers and now, by stages, into the institutions of a group of interdependent nation-states such as the European Union: a process in which the European Parliament's achievement in securing the Commission's resignation in March 1999 may come to be seen as a very significant step. I have sought, in the first and last chapters, to relate the historical experience to some of the contemporary thinking about democracy.

Warm gratitude is due to the European Cultural Foundation for its sponsorship of the project, and in particular to its President, HRH Princess Margriet of The Netherlands, who opened the conference with an address that is now the Foreword to this book. I am also grateful to the Foundation's Belgian and Netherlands National Committees, which joined the United Kingdom Committee in supporting the project, and in particular to their Chairmen, Jan-Robert Vanden Bloock and Gottfried Leibbrandt, who were unfailingly helpful, as well as to Geoffrey Denton, Director of the UK Committee, who bore the brunt of the organisational work. I am likewise grateful to Shell International and Unilever for their financial support.

The study also owes much to the advice and ideas of the participants in the conference: Lord Jenkins of Hillhead, who chaired the opening session, together with Philip Allott, Professor Herman Balthazar, Odile Chenal, Professor Hans Daalder, Ian Davidson, Geoffrey Denton, Andrew Duff, Dr Peter Kooijmans, Richard Laming, Dr Gottfried Leibbrandt, Professor Roger Morgan, Dr Paul Scheffer, J.-R. Vanden Bloock, J.H.R.D. van Rooijen, Dr H.W. van der Dunk, Stephen Woodard and, last but very far from least, the authors of the following chapters. I have learnt a great deal from their work and from their comments on the concluding chapter, for which the responsibility is, however, mine alone.

John Pinder
March 1999

The European Cultural Foundation

The European Cultural Foundation is an independent non-profit organisation founded in 1954 to promote cultural cooperation in Europe. The ECF undertakes its own projects and gives grants to other bodies for European cultural activities. It encourages the development of a pluralist civil society in Europe, linking cultural activity with social responsibility, and devises innovative cultural tools for tackling societal issues. It is also the central secretariat for two European networks: one of independent institutes for study in fields such as education, the media and the environment, and one of national committees in 23 European countries.

European Cultural Foundation
Jan van Goyenkade 5
NL 1075 HN Amsterdam
The Netherlands

Foreword

HRH Princess Margriet of The Netherlands
President of the European Cultural Foundation

The theme of this study, which is the product of Anglo-Dutch cooperation, inevitably calls to mind that earlier, fruitful Anglo-Dutch venture: I am referring to William and Mary. I hope it will not be held against me, as a descendant of the house of Orange, if I claim that the mark they left on European history cannot be ignored. I shall confine myself to those aspects of their faites et gestes which have always made the most impression on me and which I believe could serve as an example in the process of European change.

Leadership is a quality that William III undoubtedly possessed. Nor did he lack the will, armed with strong views of his own, to intervene in the major political processes of his day. But at first it was uncertain whether he would have an opportunity to express these qualities, given his precarious political status in the Republic and the international position of Holland, which was wealthy but small. Following its turbulent beginnings, the Republic of the United Provinces was able to develop in relative peace during the first decades of its existence. In addition to the creative energy and prosperity that this loose confederation manifestly generated, another important factor was that the large countries around us were too much involved in internal conflicts or in fighting one another – and often both – to make life difficult for Holland.

In 1672 this period came to an abrupt end. Nevertheless, the wars which neighbouring countries launched against the Republic in that year gave William the opportunity to emerge as a military and political leader. At the same time, the ferocity of this attempt to pluck the republican thorn from the absolutist flesh of the Sun King in particular could have put an end to our political experiment. But the great-grandson of William the Silent offered equally stubborn resistance. He went on to crown his balance of power policy – of which Henry Kissinger, in his brilliant work, *Diplomacy*, called him the founder – with the Glorious Revolution.

Leadership and willpower imply the ability to make choices, preferably sound ones. William and Mary's adoption of the Bill of Rights certainly falls into this category. Many regard it as the beginning of new political relations which led to parliamentary democracy – the present political norm in advanced societies. Cynics will be quick to point out that they had to adopt it in order to acquire the British crown. But such a view is rather too simplistic. Although centralism, absolutism and religious intolerance had far greater currency in their own day, these were practices that William and Mary did not embrace, whether in Britain or in the Netherlands.

The royal couple will also be remembered for the tone they set. Contemporaries of Louis XIV, they breathed new life into the concept of tolerance. In doing so, they created a climate conducive to the development of the institutions in which the new political relations – between sovereign and subjects, and citizens and state – are still embodied.

We should not only think about the past, however glorious it may be, but also focus on the Europe of today. The territory of the European Union now covers approximately the same area as William's balance of power policy. In the centuries after 1688, despite hopes that the balance of power could ensure stability, the European nations did not manage to conduct their political debate in a peaceful manner. Nor did later politicians succeed in creating institutions that would enable disputes to be resolved by means other than the threat of force.

That was the case until after the Second World War. Then, with the terrible catastrophes that had characterised the twentieth century at the forefront of their minds, postwar political leaders, inspired by the spiritual father of Europe, Jean Monnet, wrought a change which is just as revolutionary and just as remarkable as that brought about by William and Mary. It has, moreover, been accompanied by much less bloodshed! This new 'Glorious Revolution' made it possible to replace the traditional strategy of pursuing a balance of power – which on the whole had failed – with a policy based on justice and the rule of law.

The revolutionary concept of cooperation between nations within the European institutions has enabled Europe to enjoy peace and prosperity on a scale it had never known before. It would be useful, especially at this time, to examine the main elements of this peace formula. They include:

*   concrete socioeconomic objectives (for example, the single market);
*   (dynamic) common institutions (European Commission, European Parliament, Court of Justice);
*   procedures that promote decision-making (majority voting);
*   balanced voting powers (large countries carry more weight than smaller ones);

- one legal framework for all parties concerned: states, institutions and the public, governing all aspects of cooperation (equality before the law); and
- the will to translate this formula into practice.

I referred to several of these concepts with respect to William and Mary: sound leadership, political will, the right choices, positive climate, dynamic institutions, and justice and the rule of law. This clearly underlines their historical relevance. I would like to emphasise quite categorically that in the period prior to 1972, The Netherlands constantly campaigned for Britain's entry into the European Community, because it is precisely these concepts that we associate with the political culture that William and Mary fostered in Great Britain. They are concepts essential to any political process, including that of Europe.

Just as it is hard to turn abstract notions such as law and democracy into specific institutions to the benefit of the citizen at national level, the same is true in practice when it comes to shaping these concepts at European level. However, just as the institutions of those days, such as the Houses of Parliament at Westminster, provided a framework for fruitful development, so the European institutions of our own times enable us to advance our common interests. But institutions alone are not enough; the attitude of those who use them is equally important. That which exists has been created by people, and what has been done can also be undone.

The theme of this symposium is profoundly inspiring and I have no doubt that it will be of great value. This, of course, is precisely why the European Cultural Foundation is sponsoring the project. As the chair of the Foundation, I am confident that its impact will reverberate far beyond the confines of the original colloquium at St George's House within the hospitable walls of Windsor Castle.

1 The Development of European Democracy
John Pinder

Liberal democracy has had an extraordinary success in Europe in the second half of the twentieth century. It now prevails in the whole of Western Europe and is spreading into Central and Eastern Europe. This book seeks to throw some light, by means of a historical approach, on the process whereby this has come about.

The following chapters analyse successive stages in the development of democratic institutions. The selection of the stages is largely anglo-centric, showing the influence on England, soon to unite with Scotland to form Great Britain and later to become the United Kingdom, of the political experience of the Low Countries up to the late seventeenth century, then the influence of the British on subsequent developments. The relevance of the Low Countries' experience concerns what Robert Dahl has called 'pre-democratic institutions', including human rights, an independent judiciary, organisational autonomy together with pluralism, and a strong civil society.[1] From centuries of gestation of such institutions in Flanders and in the northern provinces that now comprise the Netherlands emerged a political culture that abhorred absolutism and, with that culture, Dutch princes were prepared to become constitutional monarchs. Thus William III was able to play the leading part in the British transition to constitutional monarchy and parliamentary government.

Although the British, like the Flemish and the Dutch, already had a long history of pre-democratic institutions, monarchs who preceded William still had absolutist pretensions. The Dutch intervention was decisive in laying the foundations for liberal democracy, with a rights-based rule of law and representative government, thus inaugurating the 'second democratic transformation' which brought democracy, from its first manifestation in the city-state of Athens in the fifth century BC, up to the level of the nation-state.[2] City-states were too small to survive as independent direct democracies; and since direct democracy was not feasible on the scale of the nation-state, it was not until royal authority was brought under the control of a representative Parliament in Britain, even if at first on a very limited franchise, that the way opened up for liberal democracy.

From Britain, the United States inherited the rule of law and representative government and combined them, consonant with a British radical tradition, with popular sovereignty, i.e. the principle that the people, not king or Parliament, were the only source of legitimate authority; and the

Americans enlarged the scope for democracy beyond the individual state by their invention of the inter-state federal system. The success of these examples of liberal democracy has been a major reason why so many European countries have come to base their polities on similar principles. The case of postwar Germany, the subject of Chapter 7, is perhaps the most striking.

The success of democratic as against absolutist institutions has indeed been remarkable. The Flemish cities and provinces were, until the repression of the absolutist Philip II, among the most advanced in northern Europe, with their pre-democratic institutions as well as in other ways. The Dutch Republic, likewise pre-democratic, was extraordinarily successful, economically, socially and culturally as well as politically. Eighteenth-century Britain was not only the cradle of the Industrial Revolution but also widely regarded as a political model, particularly in France. The influence of the United States has been enormous, in Europe and throughout the world. Postwar Germany is another outstanding example, as was, on the other side of the coin, the collapse of the Soviet system. In such circumstances, triumphalism that may seem to be implied by the use of a term such as 'the end of history' is understandable. But it is also dangerous. The history of democracy shows its development to be a process that is not likely to have an end. On the contrary, its successes lead to new challenges that constantly create a need for further development.

One such contemporary challenge is the pressure, following the growth of education and wealth in the advanced democracies, for more participatory forms of democracy. The English-language literature on the subject emphasises participation not only in the institutions of the nation-state itself, but also in local government and in economic and social organisations.[3] This follows a long-standing tradition of English writers, significantly related to continental thought. Thus Ernest Barker was strongly influenced by Otto von Gierke; and Barker was the teacher of Harold Laski, who in turn regarded Pierre-Joseph Proudhon's *Du Principe fédératif* and *De la Justice dans la Révolution* as 'two very great books'.[4] Departing from anglo-centrism, Chapter 6 concerns the French tradition of decentralist political philosophy developed by Proudhon, which goes beyond the concept of decentralised government represented by, for example, Swiss federalism, to envisage autonomous organisations down to the lowest levels in the society and the economy as well as government. Thus he applied the federal principle generally, in a way that is relevant to contemporary consideration of participative democracy.

A second challenge to contemporary liberal democracy is the fact that the boundaries of a nation-state, even a big one, are, as Dahl puts it, 'now much smaller than the boundaries of the decisions that significantly affect the interests of its citizens', thus eroding the autonomy of those states and hence the effectiveness of the democratic control of their decisions. This increase in the scale on which decisions can be effective may, he goes on, be 'as important for democracy as the change in scale from city-state to national state'; and he asks, in consequence, whether a 'third transformation' is 'now within reach'.[5] Approaching the same problem somewhat differently, Held has suggested that the interdependence, or 'interconnectedness', among nation-states should lead to a re-examination of political theory as fundamental as the shift that, from the feudal system of divided and overlapping authority, brought about 'the modern state itself'. The tension between accountability and democratic legitimacy within the nation-state and power politics beyond it has, he concludes, made it necessary to establish 'democratic public law in the international sphere as well as within states'.[6] Following a similar train of thought, Chapter 8 traces the development of the European Parliament within the European Community and Union, while Chapter 9 concludes not only with a review of the story of the second democratic transformation, to the level of the nation-state, but also with some further reflections on the European Union's pre-democratic institutions and the possibility of a third transformation, to democracy at the EU level. There can be no certainty about the destination of the European Union and its institutions. But it is to be hoped that this book will help to throw light not only on ways in which democracy can develop through stages within existing nation-states, but also on the potential for its development beyond the nation-state.

2 Mediaeval Flanders and the Seeds of Modern Democracy

R.C. Van Caenegem

On 2 March 1127 the count of Flanders, Charles the Good, was murdered in his own church in Bruges, the seat of his government, by a group of desperate conspirators, people of unfree origin whom he had threatened to reclaim as his serfs. As the count, whose father King Canute IV of Denmark had been murdered in the church of St Albans at Odense in 1086, was childless, a fierce struggle for the succession in the rich and powerful county of Flanders followed. It was won in the summer of 1128 by Thierry of Alsace, who enjoyed the support of the English king, Henry I, as against William Clito, a son of Robert Curthose, who had the support of King Louis VI of France. The deplorable murder and the ensuing bloodshed caused a deep political and constitutional crisis and much debate on the 'democratic' issues that I hope to analyse in the course of this chapter.

We are well informed on what people in 1127–28 did and even on what they thought and said about these issues, because a notary in the comital offices, Galbert of Bruges, kept a diary from March 1127 till July 1128, which is crammed with precise observations, recorded by a witness who was professionally trained to describe political and legal matters precisely and exactly.[1] Another fortunate circumstance was the date of those events. We are talking of the period made famous by Haskins's *Renaissance of the Twelfth Century* and widely recognised as the great watershed that separated the primitive, archaic, closed and thoroughly feudal early Middle Ages from the urbanised, intellectually advanced and open society of the following centuries.[2] That the Flemish crisis and Galbert's narrative are situated at the heart of that transition is a stroke of luck for, as I hope to show presently, numerous basic elements, which we associate today with democracy, then made their appearance on the scene of the historic Low Countries (i.e. roughly the present-day kingdoms of Belgium and the Netherlands, the Grand Duchy of Luxembourg and the French departments Nord and Pas-de-Calais, which formed the Seventeen Provinces under the emperor Charles V).

The rule of law

The notion of the rule of law was clearly perceived, even though it was not universally applied (when and where is this the case? Certainly not in our time) and many conflicts were settled by force of arms. Nevertheless, it is obvious from Galbert's pages that people were anxious to find out what the legal norms were and how they could be judicially imposed. When Count Charles wanted to claim the members of the Erembald clan as his serfs, he decided to bring his case before a law court.[3] And when various towns wanted to gain advantages for their citizens, they obtained borough charters (the famous keuren of Netherlandish history) in which the counts of Flanders introduced new legal arrangements.[4] These dispositions were put in writing and sealed or subscribed, as befitted proper legislative texts. In later centuries respect for the law was occasionally carried so far that the relevant article of the urban keure had to be read aloud before the law court in order to ensure its observance.[5]

One of the most striking manifestations of the respect for the rule of law is the notion that even the government must operate under the law and respect the basic legal principles that govern the state and the legitimate rights of the people. This is what we call since the early nineteenth century the Rechtsstaat or law-based state.[6] Constitutionalism, particularly when accompanied by judicial review of the constitutionality of the laws, is an important modern acquisition. Early manifestations can, however, be perceived in mediaeval Flanders, and specifically in the events of February 1128 as described by Galbert. When a comital official in Ghent attempted to re-introduce certain taxes which the new count, William Clito, had abolished, a popular revolt broke out. The count came to the city and was addressed by the leader of the opposition, Ivan of Aalst, who made a remarkable speech, duly reported by Galbert. He reproached the count for reneging on his given word and sworn promise, and thus breaking the mutual bond between him and his subjects. No prince who violated the law could legitimately continue to rule. Ivan therefore demanded that, if his accusation proved to be founded, the count should relinquish his position and give way to a ruler who respected the law. Ivan of Aalst went even further in the direction of modern constitutionalism when he proposed submitting his accusation to a court of law, composed of 'the barons from both sides, and our peers and all the responsible men among the clergy and people' and sitting at Ypres, 'which is located in the middle of your land', in order to 'judge, quietly and after due consideration, without guile or evil intent' whether the count had broken the law or not: if he had, he would have to go.[7]

Republicanism, representative assemblies and a unifying monarchy

Another democratic element which appears in Galbert – and which had a great future in the Low Countries – was government by consent. The county agreed to be ruled, but not to accept blindly whatever the prince ordained or chose to impose from above on a passive, subjected population. The government was supposed to lead the people with their consent, and had to obtain – or even to buy – their goodwill. The participation of the country in the government of the land took the form of both direct and indirect democracy. The former appeared in informal popular assemblies in open public places, where all the citizens played an active and direct part in political discussion and decision-making, and was clearly present in Galbert's day. I refer to his descriptions of popular direct action in Lille on 1 August 1127, in Saint-Omer on 3 February 1128 and in Ghent on 16 February of the same year.[8] Mass meetings in cities – orderly or unruly – became a feature of political life for centuries. One of the most fascinating examples was a popular manifestation of discontent on the Friday Market in Ghent on 29 June 1467 on the occasion of the Joyeuse Entrée of Charles the Bold: an obscure citizen, called Otto Bruneel, addressed the count in harsh and telling words, and then disappeared as quickly as he had turned up.[9]

Democracy is often associated with republicanism (it cannot co-exist peacefully with monarchy, except where the latter has come to play a symbolic, ritual role) and many of today's most successful democracies are republics. So I propose to have a look at mediaeval republicanism. It arose, as is well known, in the northern Italian city-states, where the German monarchy was rejected and urban self-governing republics founded, famous for their arts as well as their political institutions.[10] Their great competitors in northern Europe, as far as freedom and prosperity were concerned, were the Flemish cities and there also the stirrings of the republican spirit were felt, particularly so in the fourteenth century. The movement is linked to the name of James van Artevelde, whose statue stands on the Friday Market in Ghent, the very place where King Edward III was proclaimed king of France on 26 January 1340. James had become captain of Ghent in late 1337 and early 1338, at the beginning of the Hundred Years' War when Flanders, as a French fief, suffered under the embargo on English wool. The town, under an elected quasi-revolutionary leadership, rose against its count, Louis of Nevers, who sided with France. Ghent declared its neutrality, so that wool came through and the town's all-important textile industry could again feed the population.[11]

The attempt was not an isolated case in fourteenth-century Flanders, where revolts against the count and his French overlord were frequent and where it looked as if the three so-called 'quarters' of Ghent, Bruges and Ypres were turning into Italian-style city-states. It never came to that, however, and monarchical rule was made secure by the House of Burgundy towards the end of the century. But rebellion against a centralising monarchy reappeared in the fifteenth and sixteenth centuries, most notably in Ghent, where the republican heritage was never entirely lost. I refer to the Ghent revolts against Philip the Good, Charles V and – for the last time – against Philip II (from 1577 to 1584), when a Calvinist republic – with a Calvinist theological college – was established.[12] I have little doubt that this tradition of rebellion inspired the Revolt of the Netherlands against Spain and survived in the northern republic.[13] It is therefore no exaggeration to say that 'in this respect the Republic of the United Netherlands had its roots in the institutional model that had developed in Flanders and Brabant in the course of centuries of opposition to their rulers'.[14]

The road of indirect democracy was by far the more usual way of popular collaboration with the government. The representative institutions of the Low Countries – the Estates of the nobility, the clergy and the burgesses – began slowly to take shape in the fourteenth century and became a regular feature of political life. At first this happened at the level of the various provinces, such as Flanders, Hainaut, Brabant and Holland, and from 1464 onwards at the top level of the Estates General for the whole of the Burgundian Netherlands (the five-hundredth anniversary of the foundation of the Estates General was duly commemorated at The Hague in 1964).[15] From the later Middle Ages onwards there was hardly any topic occupying public opinion and concerning the general welfare, that was not discussed in the innumerable meetings between the government and the representatives of the population (the bulky documentation which they produced is being edited with great care by eminent scholars).[16] The parliamentary traditions of the Low Countries are both old and important.[17] I was told that a Dutch Member of the European Parliament had to remind a British colleague, who behaved as if Parliament was a British invention which only British politicians could run and which had to be explained to inexperienced continentals, of this fact.

The republican strain, as we have seen, never died out and was always ready to surface at moments of discontent. It certainly appeals to those modern readers who associate kings with personal rule and oppression. Constitutional monarchy can, however, be a factor of cohesion and democracy, as appears from the stable regimes of Britain, Scandinavia, Belgium and the Netherlands, and as was shown in Spain after the era of Francisco Franco. It is appropriate therefore to take a look at the positive role of the Burgundian and Habsburg monarchs in the Low Countries. It was their undeniable merit to create a new and important European state – united but not unified – where previously there had been a collection of small provincial principalities, which sometimes even fought each other. The new state of the Netherlands, which narrowly failed to become a kingdom,[18] brought greater prosperity – I mention as one of the factors the monetary union created by the New Ordinance of 1433 – and internal peace: the whole was better off than the parts and the Burgundian Netherlands had never had it so good. The cornerstone of this unity was the dynasty and the warm dynastic feeling it evoked and consciously cultivated – by the creation of the Order of the Golden Fleece, for example. This dynasty was not oppressive but lived in osmosis with its subjects.[19] One of the most romantic vignettes in the history of Ghent concerns the meeting of the Estates General on 26 January 1477, where Mary of Burgundy, who had just lost her father in the siege of Nancy, moved the members to tears with her plea for help against the threat of French annexation: they promised to be loyal 'unto death'.[20] Another, less dramatic anecdote again illustrates the people's attachment to the dynasty. When Mary of Burgundy, who had married Maximilian of Austria, produced a baby on 8 June 1478, everybody was happy because it was a boy: an important point for the continuity of the dynasty. However, some friends of France, the ancient enemy, spread the rumour that the baby was in fact a girl. So when, after the baptism at the Prinsenhof in Bruges, the people started to grumble, the young mother felt obliged to show them the young prince Philip naked and, as the chronicles put it, she took the boy's little testicles in her hand and showed them for everybody to see. So the good burghers of Bruges, seeing that it was indeed a son, were 'much relieved and full of joy'.[21] The scene reminds us of the homely paintings where the Old Flemish Masters portrayed the Holy Virgin with her baby son on her knee. What a pity Hans Memling, who lived in Bruges at the time, did not paint the picturesque scene at the Prinsenhof: it would have been the marvel of the 1994 Memling exhibition in that city.

The monarchy was the motor behind the political unification of the Low Countries, and it is not surprising that some republican cities resented this process of unification and centralisation. They saw it as a threat to their autonomy and they cherished their sovereignty, as some people in Britain today want to make a stand for British sovereignty – and especially the sovereignty of Parliament – against what they see as the encroachments of Brussels.

The legislative process

Another cardinal element of modern politics, beside Parliaments and constitutions, is the rational process of law-making and dispute settlement, and for this also we find early witness in twelfth-century Flanders. Legislation, the conscious and reasoned decision to make new laws and abolish or adapt old ones, took the place of passive and blind submission to old customs (simply because they were ancient or divinely ordained). Similarly, the law courts of the twelfth century witnessed a move away from the primitive ordeals in favour of rational enquiry into guilt or innocence.[22] It was all part and parcel of a general European leap forward from the archaic mentality, that saw the hand of God in everything, to a legal system where man took control of his destiny. Violence and revolt would give way to law and reason and to judicial procedures and peaceful argument between litigants and advocates; family feuds would be replaced by the arbitration of urban peace-makers (paiseurs, paysierders).[23]

Here again Galbert's narrative shows how early this European trend manifested itself in the Low Countries, and particularly in Flanders. When the new count William Clito wanted to win the favour of the citizens of Bruges, he granted them by way of privilege the power to change and improve their customary laws on their own authority. Clearly the burgesses believed that they – in popular assemblies or through their aldermen – could deliberately create new laws and were not obliged simply to put up with existing conditions, and they obtained the ruler's consent to go ahead with their legislative endeavours.[24] Galbert's time also witnessed the beginning of the crisis in the old irrational proofs, for in 1116 the burgesses of Ypres obtained a written charter from the count of Flanders, abolishing the ordeals of fire and water in their town.[25] Galbert mentions the 'judgement of God' very briefly, but clearly distrusts the ordeal of hot iron. He tells us how Lambert of Aardenburg, whose role in the conspiracy against Charles the Good was notorious, nevertheless managed to undergo the ordeal with success. He was, however, killed afterwards in a skirmish, so that justice was done after all. Galbert takes a jaundiced view of it all. He clearly has little faith in the ordeal as a fact finding technique, but sees it rather as a divine show of mercy to sinners and a way of pardoning their sins – at least temporarily. This does not, of course, serve the purpose of severe worldly justice, as Galbert ruefully points out.[26] The archaic ordeals were abolished in the main Flemish towns under Count Philip of Alsace, in the second half of the twelfth century, and replaced by rational means of enquiry and critical evaluation.[27]

The idea of a contract between prince and people

Popular sovereignty is another modern notion which appeared early in the history of the Low Countries. I refer, of course, to the belief that the people, and not a ruler by God's grace, wielding unlimited and unaccountable power, are the ultimate source of legitimate authority. Here again we find the earliest indications in Galbert. They are no more than timid intimations, as the monarchical principle, steeped in religion, was powerful and remained so for many centuries to come. Nevertheless, Galbert reports Flemish ideas about the role of the people in the accession of the new ruler, as against the pretensions of the French suzerain to dispose of the comital throne. He explains that on 10 April 1128, upon receiving a peremptory convocation from the king of France, the feudal overlord of the counts of Flanders, the burghers of Bruges spoke the language of defiance, and said: 'We give notice to all . . . that the king of France has nothing to do with choosing or setting up a count of Flanders. . . . The peers of the land and the citizens have the power of electing the next of kin as heir to the count's authority, and they have the privilege of raising him to the countship.'[28] It is clear that Galbert reports the first expression in mediaeval Flanders of the souveraineté nationale, to use the terminology of an article published in 1950 by the famous mediaevalist F.L. Ganshof under the title 'Les origines du concept de souveraineté nationale en Flandre'.[29] Ganshof set out to show when and in what circumstances the notion that power was owned by a prince or his dynasty was opposed to that of power belonging to the community of the free inhabitants of the country and freely delegated by them to the ruler and his descendants. He made clear that (although the term was not used) the idea of a contract between prince and people which created mutual obligations was definitely perceived. The ruler who did not abide by his duty and treated his subjects unjustly released them from their obligation of fealty. The significance of this early testimony is heightened by the fact that in 1581 exactly the same justification was given by the northern provinces when they abandoned their allegiance to King Philip II.[30]

Provincial autonomy and a federal monarchy

A last pointer to the future in Galbert's narrative concerns provincial autonomy. The federal structure of the Dutch Republic was based on respect for the autonomy of each of the seven northern provinces, which – unlike the southern ten – had escaped Spanish reconquest. In fact, one of the few express stipulations of the Union of Utrecht of 1579, which was the fundamental law of the Republic, concerned the sovereignty of the seven provinces, which were the real bearers of that of the Republic.[31] This attachment to the independence of the regions, even though they were united in a federal state, had been a permanent trait of the public law of the Low Countries ever since the Middle Ages. Here again the county of Flanders played a pioneering role, for it was the first to establish its de facto autonomy from the kingdom of France, even though (until the treaties of Madrid and Cambrai of 1526 and 1529) it never denied belonging to that kingdom.[32]

Here again Galbert's narrative came at an interesting juncture. Indeed, Flanders (like many other French regions) had broken away from (or been given up by) the West-Frankish/French monarchy ever since the end of the ninth century.[33] In the twelfth century, more precisely under Louis VI, the French crown embarked on a long-term policy of reunification. One early step in this process was Louis VI's intervention in Flanders in 1127 in order to impose his candidate for the succession of Count Charles the Good, at the very time when Galbert was writing. This first French attempt at interference in the county ended in failure, as did others afterwards. Thus the autonomy of the county of Flanders was established and preserved.[34] Something similar happened in the other Netherlandish provinces, which were situated to the east of the Scheldt (the boundary created by the Treaty of Verdun of 843) and therefore belonged to the Roman-German Empire. They – that is, Brabant, Hainaut, Holland, etc. – also loosened their links with their overlord, though much later than Flanders, and became autonomous provinces, a process that was finally recognised at the Treaties of Westphalia, when the sovereignty of the Dutch Republic was formalised.[35]

It should be understood that the Burgundian and Habsburg state of Philip the Good and Charles V fully accepted the existence of the various counties and duchies and respected their separate identities, constitutions, customs, supreme law courts and even nationalities (only natives of Brabant, for example, could hold public office there). Yet, at the same time, the dukes of Burgundy (who had entered upon their Netherlandish career through a Flemish marriage concluded in 1369) as common rulers of all these provinces also created central institutions for political, judicial, legislative and financial matters, so that a central government, at Mechelen or Brussels, and a common Parliament, the Estates General, developed. The best characterisation of that Burgundian-Habsburg state is, I believe, that of a federal monarchy. It had central institutions of government for all its lands, but did not constitute a unified nation-state, as the provinces enjoyed great autonomy and were only linked by a personal – not a real – union. It is this situation that was continued in the federal constitution of the Dutch Republic which, as is well known, found famous imitators, such as the United States of America in the eighteenth century and other important countries subsequently.[36]

It is on the foundations laid in the twelfth century that the anciennes démocraties des Pays-Bas (to quote the title of a famous work by Henri Pirenne) and the rule of law could flourish.[37] This is not the place for a comprehensive survey, so I will limit myself to two examples of their attachment to what we now call human rights: one from Flanders and one from Brabant.

In the second half of the thirteenth century the town of Bruges became involved in a protracted and costly lawsuit with its own ecclesiastical head, the Bishop of Tournai. The main issue was not the usual run of complaints about bigamy or defloration or abuse of asylum, but concerned a major aspect of what we call 'due process of law', and especially the rights of the defence. What was at stake in Bruges was the following. In the course of the thirteenth century a usage had arisen whereby parishioners, who during an episcopal visitation had been accused of some misdemeanour by the sworn 'synodal witnesses', were automatically deemed to be guilty without further proof, defence or appeal. The equation of a mere accusation with a verdict of guilty was, of course, scandalous, and only particular historical circumstances could explain how this situation had arisen. In the past the testes synodales had indeed only been a jury of indictment, whereupon the accused persons could exculpate themselves by undergoing one of the archaic ordeals mentioned earlier. However, after the Fourth Lateran Council had banned the ordeals, this defence mechanism fell away and fines were automatically imposed on accused usurers and adulterers, as if they had been duly found guilty. It was in order to obtain the abolition of this abuse that the town of Bruges sued its bishop before the official of the Archbishop of Reims. There were, admittedly, personal interests at stake, in terms of money and reputation, but it is clear that the lawsuit concerned one of the great legal principles of all civilised societies, the guarantee of a just and fair trial. The case, started in 1269 under Bishop John II of Enghien, must have ended c. 1301, probably by a compromise, in the Roman curia, to which the Bishop of Tournai, who lost his case in Reims, had appealed. It was conducted with great care, numerous witnesses being heard (as appears from the recently edited documents), and its importance to Bruges is demonstrated by the huge sums the town administration spent on it: it has been estimated that the total cost amounted almost to the yearly urban budget. The money was, however, not wasted, for the upshot of the dispute was that in Bruges, as in other towns, the following principles were introduced. The bishop had the right to appoint synodal witnesses (as proposed by the parish priest), who could accuse men and women whom public opinion deemed guilty. Afterwards the bishop had to proceed to an inquisitio, an inquest where the accused could defend themselves according to the rules of Roman Catholic canonical procedure: if no proof of guilt was established, the accused escaped with a 'canonical purgation'.[38]

The example from Brabant concerns the Charter of Kortenberg of AD 1312, a Charter of Liberties proclaimed by Duke John II which is in many ways comparable to the Magna Carta of King John (there are even some textual similarities). In Article 1 the duke promised for himself and his successors that no taxes would be imposed except in three specified cases and even then the burden of taxation was to be such that nobody was 'hurt or overburdened' (ghequetst no verlaeden). Article 2 promised that everybody would be treated according to the law and be entitled to a judicial process (houden ende setten al onse lant te wette ende te vonnesse), so that everybody, 'rich and poor', would be treated according to the existing charters. Article 4 instituted a council of supervision, comparable to the XXV barons of the English Magna Carta, composed of knights and burgesses from the main towns of Brabant.[39]

The revolt against Spanish autocracy

To a country that was used to the rule of law, free communes, parliamentary government, provincial autonomy, free discussion and the occasional urban revolt against the government, the advent of sixteenth-century absolutism – in the form of Spanish autocracy – was like a sudden and icy blast. Religious intolerance fell upon the country: no more dabbling in heretical ideas for the Chambers of Rhetoric and their famous literary tournaments! The Inquisition went hand in hand with centralisation, the Gleichschaltung of the provinces, severe taxation imposed by King Philip's personal decision and contempt for local customs and ancient urban freedoms: in short, personal rule instead of the rule of law. The result was the Revolt of the Netherlands against political autocracy and religious intolerance. The movement started in the southern Low Countries, the more populous and wealthier part, where Brussels and Mechelen were located and where the Reformation, both Lutheran and Calvinist, had made early headway. The revolt soon involved the northern parts as well and was crushed in the south by Spanish mercenary armies, first under Alva and then under Farnese. After the fall of Antwerp in 1585 the Spanish offensive came to a halt because Philip's money ran out and he had more ambitious plans on a European scale – including the conquest of England. Thus the northern provinces, the Dutch Republic, which had already valiantly resisted the Spanish onslaught (during the famous siege of Leiden, for example), escaped autocratic rule for good. What they did with their hard-earned freedom belongs to another period.[40]

The Revolt of the Netherlands was the first in a famous series of rebellions and revolutions that toppled ancient autocratic regimes. The second was the Puritan Revolution in England; the third, the American War of Independence; the fourth, the French Revolution; and the fifth, the March and October Revolutions of 1917, which together liquidated the tsarist regime.

It is noteworthy that Brinton's classic study, *The Anatomy of Revolution*, manages to forget the Netherlands and starts the series with the English events of the seventeenth century.[41] It is an illustration of the anglo-saxon blindspot which the present book seeks to remedy. Not only is the Low Countries' revolt against Spanish absolutism quite clearly at the head of the line of the great anti-autocratic movements of modern times, but it was a sort of prefiguration of the Rising of the Puritans. Indeed, it was based, as was Cromwell's movement, on two pillars: a religious concern about the true interpretation of the Gospel and a political concern about the restoration of the ancient freedoms (in England this was the common law) and the role of the representative institutions.[42]

I believe that a comparison with the English situation may be fruitful here because of the similarities and the differences. The similarities will not detain us, because they are rather obvious and stem from the fact that both England and the Low Countries belonged to the same western world: they shared the Latin Church; feudal and, in the sixteenth century, absolute monarchy; representative assemblies; respect for the legal order, and freedom under the law. There are, nevertheless, noteworthy differences. The most striking contrast is afforded by the constitutions of England and the Netherlands. England was a unitary nation-state (one of the oldest in Europe), whereas the Low Countries formed a confederation of provincial states, or at best a federal state. In England, the nation – Bede's gens Anglorum – became a state, the kingdom of Alfred the Great and his immediate successors. In the Low Countries the state – Burgundian and then Habsburg – became a nation: the dynasty produced the nationality and not the other way round.[43] Popular representation offers another contrast. The English Parliament, with its House of Lords and House of Commons, was clearly constituted by the middle of the thirteenth century.[44] The classic continental assemblies of Estates – with their three chambers of clergy, nobility and the third Estate – appear a good deal later in the Low Countries. In Flanders these Estates met for the first time in 1384; the term 'Estates' is first used in 1403 for a meeting of two Estates and in 1404 for the three Estates. This does not mean that there was no popular representation before then, but simply that it was not organised in this classic way, for a variety of reasons. The county of Flanders was previously represented by the main towns – we meet the famous scabini Flandriae in 1241 – which were so powerful that they obscured the other social groups completely. These towns came to be known as the goede steden ('good towns') and their meetings as 'Parliaments' shortly after 1300.[45]

This urban predominance explains another difference. The enthusiasm for war and military conquest under the leadership of such kings as Henry V, which involved England in the Hundred Years' War, was something the Low

Countries tried desperately to avoid. Conquest of foreign lands by Netherlandish troops, led in battle by their counts and dukes, was a most unusual sight and, as was shown under Charles the Bold, unpopular and stoutly resisted by the assemblies of Estates. When the counts of Flanders had led their knights and foot soldiers in battle, it had been during the Crusades, in the days of Thierry and Philip of Alsace and Baldwin IX:[46] very different enterprises from the conquest of Wales, Scotland or France! It is a paradox that mediaeval England, although an island, was dominated by a land-hungry military feudal class, bent on conquering more land abroad, whereas the Low Countries were mainly engaged in commercial and industrial enterprise.[47]

I would like, by way of conclusion, to widen this comparison somewhat and to pose the question as to what might explain the Flemish precocity. English and Flemish experience shows that mediaeval democracy could develop simultaneously along different lines, according to the divergent constitutions of those two lands. Thus it is clear that English parliamentary institutions were established before similar bodies in the Netherlands, but only at national level. At local and regional level there was no such precocity. The difference was, of course, caused by the fact that England was a much older nation-state than the Low Countries, so that a national Parliament could arise earlier there. On the other hand, Flanders was more urbanised and contained more powerful towns – which almost turned into city-republics – than England, where local political autonomy was unknown and where feudalism was strongly established. Consequently the earliest 'democratic' stirrings in Flanders occurred first at the local level. A similar situation arose as far as constitutionalism is concerned. Magna Carta was granted nearly a century before the Charter of Kortenberg (which concerned Brabant; there was at that time nothing like it in Flanders). But here again, the comparison should be made between the English national charter of liberties and the local charters of liberties in Flanders. As an early nation-state, England was early in obtaining a national 'constitution', whereas in Flanders grants of 'constitutions' or 'charters of liberties' (keuren) appeared a century before Magna Carta, but at the local and not at the national (Flemish, or, a fortiori, Netherlandish) level. Whether early democratic developments took place at a national or at a local level is, however, less important than that they took place at all.

This leads us to the problem of causality. Here I would like to deal briefly with the aforementioned question of how to explain Flemish precocity, and to say something on the related question of why the pioneering Italian city-republics (so similar in many ways to the Flemish towns) failed to develop political institutions that would have the same enduring influence as their Flemish counterparts. This question can only be answered in a European perspective. During the period under review the normal situation was (and is, in the modern world) that the national government was in control and that cities and boroughs operated purely at the local level, as cogs in the national administrative machinery: there is no room even for a city the size of New York exercising a (foreign) policy of its own as against the government in Washington. This 'normal' situation prevailed in England and, after some hesitation, in France, where national kings were at the helm and where, with the exception of Paris, there were no super-cities like Ghent, with its 65,000 inhabitants. In Italy, on the other hand, the opposite situation developed. The regnum Italiae in the north was ruled by a German king who was also Roman emperor. His regime was unstable, because it was foreign and almost constantly in conflict with the papacy. At the same time the general economic revival had produced several super-cities of 100,000 inhabitants, which saw a chance to go it alone and follow an independent policy in order to realise their own social and economic aims: hence the city-states. Flanders was situated between these two extremes. It knew powerful and rich cities, which profited from their geographical position and fertile fields and from the European revival of trade (which was more like Italy), but it also knew a remarkable dynasty of rulers, some of whom were powerful European princes (which was more like England and France). Consequently, when the counts were in a position of weakness (because of French pressure, or because of a struggle for the succession, as in 1127–28) the towns had the upper hand, but when strong rulers dominated the political scene (as under Thierry and Philip of Alsace) the towns behaved as subordinate parts of the county and its government.

The great parting of the ways for the Low Countries and Italy came in the fourteenth and fifteenth centuries. The Netherlandish area developed into one federal state under one common ruler – it was a quasi-kingdom. Northern Italy (which was quite distinct from the papal state and the kingdom in the south) was, on the contrary, finally divided into a number of city-states which depended nominally on the empire. In the Low Countries the old traditions of consensus and freedom flourished in the provincial Estates and the Estates General, at least until the reign of Philip II when those traditions were swamped by Spanish absolutism in the ten Habsburg provinces but survived and blossomed in the seven provinces of the Republic. In Italy the democratic phase of the end of the Middle Ages was followed by the small-scale absolutism which had turned into petty autocracies. Here the lessons of Machiavelli's *Il Principe* were heeded by local families of potentates, with foreseeable consequences for the mediaeval tradition of civic freedom, self-government and popular political culture. The same Emperor Charles V who subdued and punished rebellious Ghent in 1540 had conquered the republic of Florence in 1529, but in Italy there was no Republic of the United Provinces to take over the democratic tradition which was lost in that fateful year.

3 Republican Freedom against Monarchical Absolutism: The Dutch Experience in the Seventeenth Century
E.H. Kossmann

The complexity of the Dutch past

The tricentenary commemoration of the Glorious Revolution of 1688 was enlivened in Britain and the Netherlands by interesting celebrations and exhibitions, but it was largely ignored by the public and did not produce a great deal of scholarly discussion about the significance of the event. The commemoration of the French Revolution in 1989 was of a different scope. Over the whole world – but, of course, specifically in France – the subject was brought to the attention of the population by all sorts of means and media and, moreover, an immense output of books. Of course, the state-sponsored festivities were not without nationalist overtones but, broadly speaking, this was not a simplistic glorification of French revolutionary generosity to which the modern values of democracy and human rights were supposed to owe, if not their origin, then at any rate their first implementation. On the contrary, in influential books the ideas and events of 1789 and following years were criticised for their radicalism leading to Jacobin tyranny, terror, expansionism, imperialism and war. Yet, whatever the interpretation and evaluation of the revolution, its decisive impact on the course of world history was denied by no one.

During the commemoration of the Glorious Revolution it was suggested that 1688 was of comparable importance to 1789. Of course, it was of a different nature. It was essentially not innovative, like the French Revolution, but conservative, yet its impact was, in two respects, enormous: first, it prevented monarchical absolutism from establishing itself in Britain and building up total French dominance over the European continent; second, it achieved what it was intended for, the preservation of traditional forms of representative government, of pluralism, of tolerance, of the rule of law, of liberty. It is evident that William III, who made the revolution, brought to Britain not only a large army but also huge quantities of ingenious propaganda, thus introducing certain Dutch notions about how to rule a country in a decent as well as efficient manner. True, these notions were far from new. They had been treasured by the Dutch since the Middle Ages and kept alive thanks to the success of the Revolt of the Netherlands in the latter part of the sixteenth century. Yet, although not presented in the systematic and dogmatic style in which the French Revolution of 1789 couched its declarations, the concepts of 1688 were in actual fact no less vital. They became part and parcel of the liberal tradition prevailing in north-west Europe and deeply influenced the emerging United States.

It is not the task of this chapter to study the plausibility of the view sketched above. Its task is merely to outline the Dutch model which William III knew and of which he had learned to respect the consequences, even if they limited his freedom of action and wrecked some of his ambitions. However, to keep our interpretation in balance there is one point that should first be emphasised: the present-day kingdom of The Netherlands is not the direct heir of the governmental arrangements and political preferences functioning in the seventeenth-century Dutch Republic and thought to have been of some influence in Britain and the United States. It is rather the product of the French Revolution. At the end of the eighteenth century the Dutch Republic was no longer the vigorous state it had been in the seventeenth. When a French army attacked it in 1795 it did not defend itself. The traditional system of government collapsed, the ruling elites withdrew from their posts, new men and institutions replaced them. No violence was needed to put an end to the existence of the state which in the late sixteenth century had emerged out of the revolt. The Dutch Republic had been able to maintain itself during two centuries. In 1795 it hardly attempted to continue its life. The inhabitants, controlled but not ruled by the French victors, designed a totally new state, unitary and democratic: the very opposite of the old Republic which had been federalist and oligarchic. They took their time. Only in 1798 did they introduce a written constitution. In the first sentence it was said that through this document the Batavian people 'transformed itself into an indivisible state'.[1] Why Batavian and not Dutch? The answer is simple: the disgust of these innovators with the old order was such that even the word 'Dutch' (Nederlands) was felt to be repulsive. The name 'Netherland', one of them declared, calls up the confused image of that federal state which the new Republic has now abandoned after much struggle.[2] Much better, therefore, to go back to the very distant origins of the country when the Germanic tribe of the Batavians who resided in this area valiantly combated the Roman Empire! So it was as pristine Batavians, not as degenerate Netherlanders, that the people now at last built up the truly democratic and free state which the tyranny of stadholders and oligarchs had so long prevented them from establishing.

This Batavian episode in Dutch history did not last long. The new Republic was merely a French satellite and therefore forced to imitate the numerous political metamorphoses taking place in Paris. In 1806 the Dutch even got a king, their first since 1581 when they decided no longer to recognise the Spanish King Philip II as their legitimate ruler. This time it was a French king who governed them, the Emperor Napoleon's brother Louis: not for long, however, for after only four years he was made to abdicate and the country was incorporated into France. Yet, clearly, the two principles that after Napoleon's fall in 1813 were to characterise the once more independent Dutch state – that is, its unitary form and its monarchical structure – were both French innovations which cannot be interpreted as organically resulting out of the Dutch past. The new set-up, moreover, represented a total adaptation to the main currents of early-nineteenth-century European state-building. In the seventeenth and eighteenth centuries the Dutch state had been an exceptional phenomenon. The Dutch state of the nineteenth and twentieth centuries has little originality.

But there is, as so often in history, another side of the coin. It is by no means difficult to discover continuities between the old regime and the new system. Perceptive commentators[3] think that admittedly not the outward forms but the substance of governmental practices remind one even nowadays of old habits. During the whole history of the state, from its inception in the 1590s up to now, the Dutch desire for consensus, compromise, tolerance, and – to use a traditional term – 'mild' government has caused all constitutional forms tried out in those 400 years to adopt certain common traits. Policy-making is a slow process, preferably done in committees; the decisions eventually taken spare the options of the opponents as much as possible; pluralism and diversity are given plenty of room; humanitarian considerations prevail over appeals for harsh punishment of criminals and deviants. Principles, however firmly held, should in certain cases give way to practical prudence so that neither liberty nor power is allowed ever to break the limits of a decent society. In other words, the more or less liberal and moderate government now enjoyed by the Dutch has its roots in a long history and tradition. Thus, although the institutions changed and the old regime was abolished, the spirit running through them did not disappear so completely.

About matters such as these it is possible to carry on profound discussions that never reach firm conclusions. Fortunately, the present purpose does not require us to look for pertinent answers. One thing only needs to be stated: present-day Dutch opinion inclines to regard the arrangements of the old regime as well as those of the eighteenth-century revolution as basic elements of the nation's history which has long since absorbed both of them so deeply that they seem complementary rather than opposites. This is why the Dutch are willing to participate in the commemoration of the Glorious Revolution with as much pleasure as in that of the French Revolution.

The prince is created for the subjects

In a history of parliamentary institutions, representation, democracy, liberalism and tolerance, the Dutch state of the seventeenth and eighteenth centuries cannot be omitted. But explaining why this is so needs careful consideration. Two factors make it difficult to assess the qualities of that state. First, it was constructed in a way seemingly so strange and exceptional that to present it as a link in a grand, gradual, historical development from Middle Ages to modern times is a risky business, all the more so because it was created by a revolution (the Revolt of the Netherlands) and two centuries later, as we have seen, abolished by another one (the French Revolution). Second, we must constantly remind ourselves that certain political terms, then as well as now in current use, have in the course of time adopted different meanings, with the result that when commentators in the sixteenth or seventeenth century discussed representative government, popular sovereignty, freedom, and so on, they may well have had in mind phenomena which are at variance with the interpretation people nowadays put on these words.

The men and women who, from the 1560s onwards, took part in the troubles that much later generations decided to call the Revolt of the Netherlands did not look upon themselves as rebels, or revolutionaries, or innovators at all. On the contrary, they were convinced that they fought for the preservation of valuable traditions and customs which nobody, not even a king, had the right to disturb. Although this or similar songs have been sung in history by countless rebels in widely different situations, it is not fair or reasonable to dismiss it out of hand as empty rhetoric. The large output of pamphlets in which the actions of the so-called rebels were justified by references to ancient law and custom indicates how enormously serious and painful the problem was for faithful Christians living in fear of a God who, they knew, cursed rebels and heretics. Yet their initial position was, of course, allowed to change during the long war which ensued. In the end the opponents of the Spanish king and his servants were forced to accept that they had built up a new state which constitutionally and institutionally was very different from the late mediaeval framework and spirit they had originally put forward as their ideal exemplar. But this was not a betrayal of their former standpoints; neither was it a conversion from traditionalism to modernism. The state emerging in the 1590s was the result of circumstances, the culmination of ad hoc decisions, half-hearted solutions of intractable problems, the practical outcome of baffling events, and political theory did not yet possess instruments to attempt a proper analysis of its nature.

As a result of this it is difficult for the historian, too, to discover the true foundations of the new state, and probably it is better for him not to look for them. However, it is easy enough to determine what people wished the state not to be. It should not be an absolutist state in the form Philip II had designed: it should not be entitled to force individuals to conform to the religion which the sovereign regarded as the true one and to persecute those who refused to accept this; it should not have the right and the power to levy taxes arbitrarily, nor to suspend the ordinary processes of law, nor to encroach upon privileges that the various groups into which the population was divided – provinces, towns, guilds, urban governments, and so on – considered they had obtained in the course of time. All this had been emphasised in countless speeches, sermons, pamphlets and official documents. In January 1579 some provinces – in the first place, Holland and Zeeland – that were deeply concerned by the military and political successes of the great Spanish general, Parma, decided to concentrate their forces more adequately than before in order to pursue the war and thus concluded the so-called Union of Utrecht, of which eventually only the seven northern provinces were the members.[4] In the seventeenth and eighteenth centuries this document was used as a fundamental law of the Republic, although it was not intended to be anything of the sort and the most important innovations introduced by it were never put into effect. We may characterise the Union of Utrecht as a formal alliance of provinces acting as if they were independent states, and deciding to integrate their foreign policies and war efforts through a fairly loose federation in order to defend their individual independence and traditional customs. It is noteworthy that the first article, according to which the provinces should hold together as if they were only one province, goes on to state that the purpose of this is to preserve their separate identity. Another element that needs emphasis is the short passage about religion. The religious issue was of decisive importance. Given the circumstances of that moment it would have been totally unrealistic to try to transform the Union into a purely Protestant association. In this matter, too, the final decisions about the religious regime to be installed in the various provinces were left to themselves. But in all of them, individuals would enjoy freedom of conscience and no one could be prosecuted or questioned about his or her religion. The only principle held to be universally valid in 1579 was that all inhabitants of the northern Netherlands were free in their conscience and none of them could be forced to conform to whatever religion was declared by the authorities to be the right or the dominant one.

A second fundamental document that exemplifies the spirit of those who were half-unwittingly building up a new state is the so-called Act of Abjuration of 1581.[5] This is a resolution of the States General, then meeting at The Hague, which forbade the inhabitants to obey Philip II any longer because, in the course of the years, he had proved to be a tyrant and, being an enemy of the people, had forfeited his sovereignty. There was nothing very dramatic about this document. It was written in a flat style: no rhetoric or lofty generalisations accompanied the argumentation which explained why it was from now on illegitimate for the inhabitants to regard Philip II as their sovereign. It was not a declaration of independence, for nothing whatsoever was said about the future form and authority of the provinces assembled in the States General. The text did not indicate what the States General thought had happened to the sovereignty Philip had been gradually losing. This was clearly not meant as a statement of principle initiating the construction of a non-monarchical independent state. Nor did it operate in such a way, for, in the next few years, the Dutch seriously attempted to order their hopelessly complicated affairs by introducing a new monarchical form of government, ruled by a local dignitary – William of Orange himself – or by a foreign prince. All these attempts collapsed. Yet they were extremely interesting because they, or some of them, led the Dutch negotiators to draw up treaties which the prospective new sovereign should approve before being accepted as such. In these draft treaties we see the Dutch explore the possibility of couching in precise, juridically correct language the outline of what in later history was to become the constitutional parliamentary monarchy – the outline only, for essential features of it were not yet within the grasp of this generation: sovereignty, representation, 'people', were often mentioned, but hardly ever were the content and the nature of these concepts further defined. The spirit of this all, however, was perfectly clear. It was in total harmony with the few generalisations with which the Act of Abjuration starts: 'It is common knowledge that the prince of a country is appointed by God to be the head of his subjects to protect and shield them from all iniquity, trouble and violence . . . and that the subjects are not created for the benefit of the prince . . . but that the prince is created for the subjects.' If the prince acts tyrannically he must no longer be obeyed and in his stead another must be elected to be an overlord called to protect them.

During the 1580s the Dutch failed to find in Holland, France or England a new sovereign willing and able to play this role. They stood alone, and from the late 1580s onwards they felt themselves strong enough to accept this, and thus to accept, too, that their state was an independent republic. How must we characterise this state? Superficially it had the appearance of late-mediaeval arrangements with representative assemblies, the provincial States, in each of the seven provinces and a federal assembly, the States General, where members of all the provinces met regularly to decide upon common matters. The main difference from the old situation was that the provinces had lost their sovereign ruler, Philip II, who had been duke in Guelderland, count in Holland and in Zeeland, *etcetera*. As a result, the provinces, no longer connected with each other in a personal union, had regained much of their mediaeval autonomy. In such an interpretation the new Republic, product of a conservative revolution, seems to possess strangely old-fashioned qualities and to represent a retrogressive rather than a progressive episode in the history of European state-building. Somewhat closer inspection, however, shows this view to be misleading. Most certainly the Dutch Republic was not a state constructed on clear and systematically ordered new principles. Yet that it was a highly original state with a constitution and institutions still carrying the traditional names, but in fact widely different from their mediaeval predecessors, cannot be denied.

The States and the stadholder

It is not necessary in this chapter to describe the institutions in any detail;[6] some short notes on their working are nevertheless required before it will be possible to answer the question of whether or not we may use terms like 'representative assemblies', 'popular sovereignty' or 'democracy' when trying to characterise this state and its values. The central organ of the Republic was the States General in which seven provinces were represented, the province of Holland with Amsterdam, The Hague and Leiden being by far the most important economically, politically and culturally. Each of these provinces sent as many representatives to the States General as it wanted or as the limited space of the meeting room in The Hague permitted. But each possessed only one vote and the representatives were bound to vote as instructed by the States of their respective province. In important matters there was in theory no question of out-voting the minority since unanimity of the seven sovereigns was required for taking a decision binding on all of them. In practice, however, a majority decision was carried out notwithstanding the opposition of one or more of the provinces. These were often later on persuaded or forced to approve, nevertheless. A famous case was Zeeland's refusal in 1648 to subscribe to the Peace of Munster while allowing it to be officially proclaimed in its territory. The States General met every day, even on Sundays, for a couple of hours. Their importance was considerable. They acted as the representatives of the Union, conducted foreign policy, controlled defence and the federal taxes which were apportioned among the provinces according to a strict scheme. Holland paid almost 60 per cent of them. But although the power of the States General should not be underestimated, it was nevertheless strictly limited. There was no federal court of justice, no federal Church government, no federal internal administration in general. Provincial sovereignty was carefully respected and it was difficult for any of the federal organs drastically to encroach upon provincial rights.

If in practice the Republic possessed a far greater unity than this federal system would seem to allow, this was due to the overwhelming power of the province of Holland. In Holland, as in all the other provinces, it was the States that were supposed to possess sovereignty. The various provincial States, or representative assemblies, were not, however, organised in an identical manner. Holland's system was as follows. The States had 19 members, each of them having one vote. One vote belonged to the nobility, 18 to the most important towns of the province. In major matters unanimity was required. The States met at least four times a year for a few weeks, up to a total of over 150 days in times of stress. The daily work was done by a standing committee of approximately ten members appointed for a number of years. As the urban delegations to the States were composed of men belonging to the urban regent families, that is, the local patricians of non-noble extraction, it is clear that the provincial government was largely in control of this very small group. The States had few salaried officials. By far the most important among these was the so-called Raadpensionaris, which means 'salaried councillor' but who is usually called 'Grand Pensionary' in English. He was also the salaried councillor of the nobility and in that capacity he acted as chairman of the States of Holland and of their committees and as the leader of the Holland deputation to the States General. But although it was out of traditional respect for the nobility that its councillor was charged with these superior responsibilities, the Grand Pensionary himself was not a nobleman and drew his often decisive influence in essence from his role as spokesman of the urban patriciate to which he belonged.

The position of the stadholder was still more complicated. As he was appointed by the States of the various provinces, his was legally a provincial function dependent on the sovereign will of his principals. Several elements, however, bestowed on the incumbent of the office a far higher status. The dignity derived great importance from the fact that in Holland, Zeeland and most of the other provinces, only the princes of Orange, heirs to the immensely popular tradition of William the Silent, were appointed as stadholders. Moreover, thanks to his being stadholder in various provinces at the same time, the Prince of Orange, though not a member of the States General, naturally participated in the making of federal policies. As he often also held the functions of captain-general and admiral-general of the Union, his activities were, in fact, never confined to merely provincial matters. The stadholdership itself included several truly sovereign rights which had formerly belonged to the stadholders of Burgundian times who often acted as the substitutes, the locum tenentes, of the distant sovereign. The stadholders of the Republic possessed the right of electing urban magistrates and appointing several provincial officials. They sometimes exercised the right of granting pardon or remission of penalties, although various provincial States also claimed and in effect monopolised it. Often the stadholdership was regarded by contemporaries as the monarchical element in a state with a mixed constitution. This was certainly an inaccurate way of describing the structure of the Republic, but it had the merit of indicating that, notwithstanding the legal supremacy of the States, actual practice as well as its theoretical rationalisation needed the help of different powers and conceptions. From the sociological point of view it is clear that the presence of this princely tradition helped to mitigate the absolute character of the ruling oligarchy, though it should be added that the princes of Orange were rarely willing and never able to supersede the Holland plutocracy, from whom they and the Republic ultimately received the money they needed and the directives motivating their policies. Thus William III of Orange was used to working with assemblies that had 'the power of the purse' and was, when he became William III of England, prepared to accept that the Westminster Parliament too should possess that essential power.

Both during the ancien régime itself and later among its historians, there has been much discussion about the value of this system of government. Some commentators have deplored its inefficiency and ambiguity. Prominent Dutch scholars – the most renowned Dutch historian of the nineteenth century, Robert Fruin (1823–1899), among them[7] – considered the Republic, notwithstanding their admiration for its greatness in the seventeenth century, as a fundamentally regrettable interruption of a development which, if it had been allowed to follow its natural and logical course, would have led the Burgundian monarchy gradually to transform itself into the best conceivable system of government: that is, the nineteenth-century liberal and constitutional monarchy. In other words, the emergence of the Republic prevented the Dutch state from taking the straight road towards the liberal ideal along which Britain had been able to go. In the late eighteenth century the Dutch experiment ended in total failure. The British method triumphed. And, remarkably enough, even France was thought by some to have been wiser by associating itself with the tendency dominating historical evolution and uniting the nation at an early stage by means of vigorous absolutism. In the view of such commentators, even Louis XIV had his merits.

There are at least two reasons why historians nowadays feel no sympathy with this sort of speculation. The first is obviously that they have generally become sceptical about such grand theory and less inclined to claim to know who in the past read the historical map correctly and as a result took the right direction. Moreover, and this is the second reason, they do not contrast the working of the Dutch institutions with that of the great monarchies of the time in such vivid colours as historians of former generations used to do. Our perspective has changed. Much research has shown that in spite of all monarchical splendour and absolutist rhetoric, seventeenth-century governments generally were inefficient and did not penetrate deeply into society. If the Dutch form of government might look disorderly, at any rate from the standpoint of the modern historian, so did the French or the English one. Yes, there is reason to regard the Dutch system as better adapted to seventeenth-century circumstances. It left local government which had direct contact with the population more room than Parisian absolutism, which made it easier to deal with the widespread popular unrest of this age. And if serious conflicts arose within the central governments themselves, as they did at various times in the Republic, in England and in France, the very ambiguity of the Dutch system made it possible to act more cautiously than the more rigid French and English arrangements, and thus to avoid outright civil war and violence. Finally, the presence of provinces and towns in the assembly halls of the federal institutions permitted them to bring local needs and desires to the attention of the major statesmen. On the whole, the Dutch government was more flexible and, particularly in economic matters, more creative than its European counterparts. This is the view of competent historians. It is very convincing as far as the days of Dutch greatness are concerned, but during the long period of Dutch decline in the eighteenth century it simply does not work. What we may praise as the merits of the constitution in the seventeenth century must be regarded as its flaws in the eighteenth.

Sovereignty and oligarchy

The preceding considerations suffice, it is hoped, as an introduction to the analysis of the concepts under discussion: sovereignty, democracy and representation. It was painfully difficult for the Dutch to define the meaning of these terms in the circumstances that confronted them. Take sovereignty. After 1581 nobody living in the provinces represented in the States General was allowed any longer to recognise Philip II as his sovereign. Five years later, in 1586, the States for the first time claimed that sovereignty was not merely provisionally held in trust by them until a new sovereign would be appointed, but now actually resided with them. This entitled them to bestow on the Earl of Leicester, sent by Queen Elizabeth to help the Dutch, much more power than the extremely cautious queen, who was reluctant to involve herself too deeply in the war against Spain, had wished him to exercise. After Leicester's definitive departure in December 1587, sovereignty was thought to reside firmly with the States, but whether one should look upon the States of the individual provinces or upon the assembly of all these institutions in the States General as the true bearers was not fully clear before the middle of the seventeenth century when the issue was decided in favour of the provincial States. But there was a still more fundamental problem regarding sovereignty that worried the Dutch: its origin.

This question, too, became acutely relevant during the short and unhappy Leicesterian period.[8] The Earl arrived in the beginning of 1586. In November 1586 he returned to England for a couple of months, leaving behind him a number of English agents to carry out his orders. One of them was Sir Thomas Wilkes, a diplomat about 41 years of age with great experience in international affairs. It was his task to persuade the States of Holland and the States General to support Leicester's policies which they had come to resent and to resist. For this purpose he wrote in March 1587 a memorandum[9] – in French – in which he sharply criticised these institutions for claiming to possess sovereignty. In the absence of a legitimate prince, Wilkes stated,

> the sovereignty belongs to the commonalty and not to you, gentlemen, who are only servants, ministers, and deputies of the commonalty and have commissions which are limited and restricted not only in time but also in subject matter. These are conditions as widely different from sovereignty as is the power of the subject from that of the prince or of the servant from that of the master, or, to express it more clearly, as heaven from earth, for sovereignty is limited neither in power nor in time. Still less do you represent sovereignty.

Wilkes's point was that not the States had appointed Leicester to his governorship, but the sovereign people. The States were merely agents of the people, totally dependent on the people's will. As it was by no means obvious that the people wanted Leicester's power to be curbed, the States acted illegally by opposing him.

The States of Holland took Wilkes's memorandum seriously. In the tense situation in which they found themselves, threatened by the foreign enemy and by explosive internal controversy, they considered it necessary to commission a gifted jurist, Franchois Vranck, then about 31 years old, to expound their own view on the problem of sovereignty in the Netherlands. This document,[10] approved by the States in October 1587, became a classical statement the main tenets of which were adopted by all Dutch writers who, in the seventeenth and eighteenth centuries, tried to justify the local system of government. Vranck agreed that the concept of popular sovereignty was the principle of Dutch government but made it clear that the Englishman was mistaken in his view that the States consisted of mere individuals appointed by the people to carry out the people's wishes. Vranck pointed out that the States were not just a group of individuals but an institution, an organised and organic body of men, a centuries-old, stable, unchanging assembly rooted in history, that did indeed not represent the people in the sense that its members were elected by the people with a clear mandate, but nevertheless was truly popular because in a deeper sense it was the people itself. It is the towns' magistrates and councillors and it is the corporation of the nobility that send delegates to the States which thus consist mainly of urban patricians to whom, as a group, superior authority had in some remote past apparently been confided by the population at large. In other words, if the States of Holland rightly claim to possess sovereignty it is not the individual members who do so, but the assembly as such, and all the other authorities involved in indicating the persons who must become members of the States. The main point, however, of Vranck's argument was that the States of Holland had, from time immemorial, during at least eight centuries, possessed sovereignty.

To the modern mind, an argument like this is unconvincing. The historical exposition provided by Vranck was wrong, and to claim that the system sketched by him was founded on popular sovereignty may strike us as preposterous. Yet for two centuries, well educated men appreciated this as a satisfactory view of their system of government. The point is that for them and the Calvinist authors from whom both Wilkes and Vranck drew their inspiration, 'people' was not, as for us, the totality of all adult individuals in possession of civil rights living in a state. For them, 'people' was an organic whole, an organised group of men participating in the government of towns, or countryside, or provinces, or the Republic as a whole. Those who did not do so were mere individuals, and the totality of those individuals did not constitute the people but a 'populace' or multitude. In practice this meant that it was by no means necessary for a state whose authority was considered to be derived from popular sovereignty to be democratic in the modern sense of the word.

In fact, as our survey of Dutch institutions has indicated, there was hardly any trace of democratic participation in government left in the Republic. The system was thoroughly oligarchic. In the course of the seventeenth century, intelligent Dutch commentators sometimes went so far as to equate the fullness of power possessed by the provincial States with that of absolute kings. This may not have been enlightening for even if the theory had some substance in practice the exercise of that power was surely widely different, yet it gives the question left for further consideration a new dimension. How, in effect, should we assess the quality of the Dutch institutions in their capacity of representative assemblies? And if they possess absolute power, how then do they compare with the British eighteenth-century Parliament, on behalf of which the same claim has been made by some? The answer to these questions has been given implicitly in the synopsis of the institutional framework. It is clear that the provincial States of Burgundian and Habsburg time did indeed represent the various groups into which the population had been traditionally divided: clergy, nobility and the third estate (although there was a lot of variety: the nobility, for example, being excluded in Flanders, and the clergy in Holland and Guelderland). The task of these was to help the sovereign by giving advice and granting subsidies. After the Spanish reconquest of the southern provinces the situation there returned to its old pattern. In the northern provinces this was not so. There the representative assemblies became sovereign rulers themselves. It was they that governed the provinces and the country, sometimes in conjunction with the stadholder but, from 1650 to 1672 and from 1702 to 1747, when Holland had no stadholder, quite independently, and never did any stadholder of Holland, however influential, assume the role of a king. This suggests that in republican times the Dutch system cannot be characterised as representative. To say that nobility and towns in Holland were represented in the States is fundamentally meaningless. The members of the States belonged exclusively to the families ruling the towns. This was a division of labour rather than a representation. The difference with Britain is obvious. The Dutch arrangement did not provide for elections but only for certain rules regulating the distribution of offices among the patricians by a system of cooptation. It did not produce a proper government or a ministerial Cabinet. And it had no room for a king. If it is true that the British institutions paved the way for the development of present-day representative democracy, the same cannot be said of the Dutch.

The success of freedom

And yet, the United Provinces were undoubtedly a most important element in the complicated range of factors that gradually led to the emergence of the modern state. The very fact that in the time of its greatness the decentralised Republic was able to survive disasters of tremendous proportions, such as the coordinated attack by the kings of France and England in 1672, drew the attention of Europe to this exceptional society, more prosperous than any other European nation and ruled in a manner unprecedented in history and incomparable in its own day. The practical success of such a state generated much commentary, both critical and laudatory. Add to this the spectacle of a measure of religious and intellectual tolerance unimaginable in the rest of Europe and one sees why contemporaries and later observers studied the Republic carefully, first for its achievements, and then, in the late eighteenth century, for its indisputable decline. Obviously, there was a connection between the institutions of the Republic and the liberal character of its society. This chapter, however, would burst out of its seams if it were to take on the task of describing in any detail how the governmental system was used both by rulers and inhabitants as a means to protect or promote the liberties the Dutch had fought for during the Revolt. The point is that its very complexity and the immense variety of customs, regulations and arrangements operating in the seven sovereign republics, their numerous towns and their countryside, all treasuring their old traditions (real or imagined), often prevented uniform legislation from being issued either on the federal or the provincial level or, if it was actually issued, from being effective. This created room for a form of pluralism decried by foreign absolutists as anarchy and disorder but cherished by the Dutch as liberty.

Indeed, both in the perception of the Dutch themselves and of the foreigners visiting the country or reading about it, one of the main characteristics of that society was the dominant value attached to freedom. Freedom was thought to constitute the very basis of the Dutch state in four respects: first, freedom meant independence of the federal Republic as a whole; second, it also meant the sovereign status of each of the seven provinces forming the Republic; third, it meant that the stadholder in the various provinces, though often a powerful statesman, should not become a sort of king, republicanism being a better form of government than monarchy; finally, the principle of freedom of conscience which had been clearly defined in the basic text to which Dutch writers about the constitution constantly referred, the Union of Utrecht of 1579, was an inviolable element of Dutch life. These four freedoms, which we can see gradually developing in the course of the late sixteenth and the seventeenth centuries, were finally regarded as a coherent whole as if the Dutch concept of freedom was comprehensive and consecrated by the nation's immemorial tradition. Freedom was praised as the leading principle of the Dutch Republic in all spheres of human endeavour, religious and economic as well as political, and it was therefore essentially the same freedom which manifested itself in all those fields. The four freedoms mentioned were interpreted as fundamentally belonging together in an organic whole. In reality, of course, this was not so, as is easily shown by the simple fact that all of them did not originate at the same moment and they developed rather haphazardly as a result of unforeseen and totally unplanned circumstances. Yet the view was impressive and has at least the enormous merit of giving a plausible explanation of a society that baffled contemporaries abroad, and sometimes even at home.

By way of a conclusion, the following statements may perhaps be risked. First, although the structure of the Dutch Republic was not representative in the modern sense of the word and, notwithstanding its claim to be based on the concept of popular sovereignty, was by no means democratic, it could nevertheless convincingly be used as proof of the fact that a non-absolutist form of government worked more satisfactorily than absolute monarchy, and achieved more prosperity and a much better civil discipline and order. Second, although the idea that Dutch seventeenth-century society was inspired by a single coherent principle of freedom can be shown to be an a posteriori interpretation of a fundamentally unprincipled practical set of unexpected circumstances, the myth, if it must be so called, had the merit of equipping the practice of freedom with a nice intellectual justification, with the result that the Dutch experience not only showed that liberty was an excellent tool to keep a complicated and dynamic society going, but also provided a solid foundation for a new philosophy of liberal government.

4 William III, the Glorious Revolution and the Development of Parliamentary Democracy in Britain

Jonathan I. Israel

During the second half of the seventeenth century, Britain, together with Ireland, was regarded in Europe, with no small justification, as being more divided politically, more unstable and more prone to revolution than France, Spain, Germany, Italy or any other major European country of the time. The spectacle of the English Civil War of the 1640s, the execution of Charles I, Cromwell and the English republic of the 1650s, the Restoration of 1660, and not least the Rye House Plot of 1683 when the Whig leadership, in reply to mounting royal pressure, conspired to seize the king and take control of the realm, leading to the arrest and trials of many leading Whigs, the flight into exile of others, and the execution of Lord Russell and of Algernon Sydney, one of the leading Whig ideologues of the period: all these seemed compelling evidence of the fundamental turbulence of England's political life and culture. Meanwhile, both Scotland and Ireland were likewise deeply divided in politics and constitutional matters as well as religion.

Especially in England this state of dividedness was not only a matter of practical politics and ecclesiastical organisation but also ideological and, in the broadest sense, philosophical.[1] On the one side stood those who adhered to what became known as 'Tory principles', based essentially on divine right absolutism and mirroring the social and cultural attitudes which then prevailed in most of continental Europe: the notion that it is sinful to resist the authority of the king who is anointed by God and proclaimed by the public Church, on whatever pretext, and which went together with a strong preference for religious uniformity and a hierarchical, aristocratic view of society, as well as the idea that established authority of whatever kind derives its legitimacy from God's will. On the other side stood the opposing Whig ideology, which showed a consistent preference for republican attitudes and ways of thinking, for toleration and religious pluriformity,[2] and for the idea of authority of whatever kind deriving its basic legitimacy from the people's consent, and which accepted constitutional arrangements and (according to some) an underlying social contract. These rival sets of principles undoubtedly also corresponded to opposing and competing models of how society should properly and best be organised. On the one hand stood the sort of absolutism, with its informal methods of making the main decisions in the state, stress on uniformity in belief and thought, tight censorship and courtly, aristocratic outlook and culture – which at that time flourished most impressively and persuasively in France – and, on the other, the consultative, less hierarchical and more tolerant model, associated above all with the Dutch Republic. That the competing political elites of Britain were acutely aware of the wider European context in which these warring sets of principles were at work is evident from a rich variety of evidence, including an amusing anecdote concerning Anthony Ashley Cooper, the third Earl of Shaftesbury, in conversation at Amsterdam with a Dutch regent during the late seventeenth century: 'There is no need I should tell you', observed Shaftesbury, 'that in all our nation the only lovers of Holland are the lovers of liberty called Whigs. The contrary party (the Tories) are inveterate and I remember a saying of one of the best and wisest of our latter Patriots who used often to give it out for a rule, if you would discover a concealed Tory, Jacobite or papist, speak but of the Dutch and you will find him out by his passionate railing.'[3]

There is little doubt, moreover, that this chronic political instability and deeply embedded ideological strife so characteristic of the British scene in the late seventeenth century did not suddenly cease overnight with the Glorious Revolution of 1688–89.[4] On the contrary, the new regime which came in in 1689 had, at best, only a precarious grip on power down to the summer of 1690 and, even after that, continued to face formidable opposition in England as well as Ireland and Scotland, at least down to the middle of the 1690s.[5] After that, the position did stabilise and, as the eighteenth century proceeded, the old image of a profoundly divided, strife-torn, fiercely ideological England rapidly faded, the bitter war of principles slowly lapsed, and an entirely new image of England as a proud, united constitutional monarchy, with Parliament rather than the crown the dominant partner in government, and the fount of authority and law, increasingly became established.

The change was indeed far-reaching and of profound consequence and, contrary to what one school of historians continues to argue,[6] can be said to demonstrate the centrality of the Glorious Revolution in British history. Not that the arguments of the so-called 'revisionists' are entirely wrong. Not at all. For a strange paradox emerges from the recent historiography of the Glorious Revolution. Thus almost all the individual planks of the old Whig view of the Glorious Revolution have been shown to be largely mistaken: the notion that the revolution was the culmination of a long struggle for constitutional rights and liberties, as well as religious toleration, which most of the population supported; the assumption that the English carried the process through basically on their own initiative, with Parliament taking the lead and virtually the entire nation joyfully accepting the outcome of the revolution. Yet the underlying Whig conviction that the Glorious Revolution was an event of decisive, fundamental, overarching significance in British history can, nevertheless, on excellent grounds be accepted as correct.[7] Nor is it any less the case that almost every plank of the revisionist argument is cogent, well founded and has to be accepted: the claim that the late Stuarts had much stronger and more extensive support for their policies and encountered greater acquiescence in their rule than the Whig interpretation would have us believe; that in reality there was relatively little support in the country for the Glorious Revolution either at the outset or at a later stage, at least before the late 1690s; that Parliament played only a passive and largely subordinate role during the crucial opening phase of the revolution; and that without large-scale Dutch intervention in Britain there would have been no Glorious Revolution at all. Yet the conclusion which the revisionists have drawn from all this, that the Glorious Revolution has been greatly overrated as an event and was really a rather marginal occurrence, is, notwithstanding all these revisions, fundamentally wrong.

Doubtless there were various reasons why the strangely muted tercentenary celebrations of 1988–89 failed to make much impact in Britain, or get across the message that the Glorious Revolution was of crucial significance in the evolution not just of modern Britain but of the entire English-speaking world and beyond. In the first place, some historians, the 'revisionists', do not believe it was as fundamental as others say it was and argue against the claims made by the latter. Second, as a number of observers had noted, there were strong inhibitions about discussing the Glorious Revolution in its Irish context since in Northern Ireland it remained a divisive symbol, remembered as a civil war which ended in the conquest of the Catholics by the Protestants backed by a large Anglo-Dutch army; and its significance in the development of parliamentary democracy and constitutional monarchy was largely ignored, as was also William's commitment to religious tolerance. But a third reason which might be pointed out is that the planners organised the tercentenary celebrations on a joint Anglo-Dutch basis and presented the Glorious Revolution as an Anglo-Dutch affair without making it the least bit clear that the Dutch involvement was, in reality, far more fundamental and far more complex than simply a dynastic one based on the fact that William III of Orange was a nephew of Charles II and James II and the husband of James's daughter, Mary. On the contrary, the strategy was to stress monarchy, albeit in its constitutional form, and the dynastic link, as if what chiefly mattered then, as today, were the connections between the British and Dutch royal dynasties. By overstating the dynastic factor and, for the most part, leaving out of the picture the political and constitutional aspects of the Dutch intervention in Britain and Ireland, there was, in my view, a crucial failure not just of historical interpretation but also of publicity and presentation of history to the public.

Historians are now more willing than they used to be to accept that the change of regime which occurred in Britain and Ireland in 1688–89 occurred, and occurred only, because a large Dutch army under the command of William III and including a strong auxiliary force of Whig exiles and Huguenots landed in England and marched on London, and because the English royal army, able to concentrate only about 12,000 not very well-trained men against William's more experienced, better equipped and more powerful army of 21,000 men, was simply too weak to oppose the invasion.[8] As the authority of James II crumbled, the Prince of Orange ordered all the royal regiments and guards in London to remove themselves from the capital; and the whole of London, including the royal palaces and every part of Whitehall, was placed under Dutch military occupation which continued throughout the crucial winter of 1688–89 and for many months thereafter.[9] The long silence about the invasion of Britain and military occupation of London which has so long been characteristic of Glorious Revolution historiography has now definitely come to an end. But it is striking that this fact, that the revolution was triggered by a military invasion and carried through in a London occupied by a Dutch army and from which all royal troops had been sent away, has so far chiefly been used by the 'revisionists' in order to de-emphasise the revolution's constitutional importance in the making of modern Britain. The logic here seems to be that if the constitutional opposition to James II was not in reality either as strong or as active in the making of the revolution as the old Whig interpretation alleges, and if Dutch intervention was militarily decisive, as clearly it was, then the subsequent radical changes in the relationship between crown and Parliament – the permanent strengthening of Parliament, the introduction of a formal toleration by parliamentary statute, and the entire post-1689 political culture of constitutional balance and decision-making by consultation and parliamentary committees – must have come about through other circumstances hardly connected with the revolution of 1688–89 as such.

In particular, it is often argued nowadays that it was really England's involvement in the Nine Years' War (1688–97) against France, and the huge rise in recruiting, spending and taxation which that participation brought about, and not the revolution of 1688–89 as such, which led to a permanent change in the balance and the nature of the relationship between crown and Parliament. Another, allied strand of argument which calls into question the centrality of the Glorious Revolution in the rise of the British parliamentary system is the contention that, while William originally espoused the cause of constitutionality in his publicity and propaganda, and especially in his published *Declaration* of October 1688, very soon, once James's power collapsed and the Prince of Orange was within sight of the throne, the 'Orange camp began to distance itself from its original manifesto' and stress not the 'rights and liberties' of Englishmen but the role of William as the instrument of a providential God intervening in the Protestant cause.[10] Looked at in this light, the Williamite message can be presented as something thoroughly ambiguous, more concerned, from late 1688 or early 1689 onwards, with a providential rhetoric as apt, or more so, to 'ally with extensive claims for royal power' than with a parliamentary ideology. But the stadholder-king could not so easily detach himself – assuming that he would have wished to – from the publicity, discourse and propaganda that had been so massively put to work in the early stages of the revolution. Back in Holland, he and his entourage had sought to maximise the chances of success in Britain, in the autumn of 1688, by means of a carefully prepared propaganda campaign which they planned to mount on an unprecedented scale. Both William's main *Declaration* to the English people, and his separate *Declaration* for Scotland, had been intricately drafted and crafted and when ready had been printed in enormous quantities in The Hague, Rotterdam and Amsterdam several weeks before the invasion armada set out from Hellevoetsluis. The stocks of copies were kept secret until the last moment when they were suddenly released, and poured by the thousand into the public consciousness, in every part of Britain and even in New England; one of the most active distribution centres in London, remarkably enough, being the Spanish embassy.[11] The public reading of the Prince of Orange's *Declaration* formed the climax of the revolution in many English provincial towns, including Manchester, Chester, Durham, Leeds, Oxford and Plymouth, as well as Exeter, which was the first town entered by the invading army. Subsequently, the Prince himself never failed to emphasise the con-stitutional stance he had set out in his *Declaration* whenever embarking on some further step in his assumption of power in Britain. Thus, in his open letter to both houses of Parliament of 22 January 1689, the Prince announced that he did not doubt 'but that by such a full and free Representative of the Nation, as is now met, the Ends of my *Declaration* will be attained'.[12] A few months later, in 'His Majesties Gracious Letter to the Meeting of the Estates in His Ancient Kingdom of Scotland', of 17 May 1689, William observed that on embarking on his expedition to Britain, 'we had particular consideration and regard for Scotland, and therefore we emitted a *Declaration* for that, as well as this Kingdom, which we intend to make good and effectual to you, and you shall always find Us ready to protect you and assist you in making such Laws as may secure your Religion, Liberties, and

Properties . . .'.[13] In his most gracious speech to both houses of the English Parliament of 4 November 1692, the stadholder-king thanked the assembly 'for the great supplies you have given me for the prosecution of this war', and once again assured MPs that 'I am sure that I can have no interest but what is yours; we have the same religion to defend, and I cannot be more concerned for the preservation of your liberties and properties than I am that you should always remain in the full Possession and Enjoyment of them'.[14] The *Declaration* of October 1688 was undoubtedly regarded as the definitive statement of James II's subversion of the constitution but also was generally seen as having introduced, and paved the way for, the Bill of Rights. Thus, in the Bill of Rights, the Lords and Commons expressly state 'to which Demand of their Rights, they are particularly encouraged by the Declaration of his Highness the Prince of Orange, as being the only means for obtaining a full redress and remedy therein'.[15] If later it came to be forgotten in Britain that it was William's *Declaration* which had led to the introduction of the Bill of Rights, during the 1690s the English public were still intensely conscious of this.[16]

The fact that Parliament did not take the lead in the making of the Glorious Revolution and that the decisive impetus came from outside rather than from within most certainly does not mean that therefore the entire episode is secondary, or other than fundamental, in the transformation of Britain from a late Stuart would-be absolutist monarchy into a firmly constitutionalist 'crowned republic'. The Glorious Revolution in Britain was, to be sure, essentially the product of a wider play of forces in Europe involving the expansionism and ambitions of Louis XIV and the defensive strategies of the Dutch Republic and the German Protestant states, as well as the Emperor, but this does not preclude its having been a crucially formative episode in the history of Britain.[17] On the contrary, it is my view that a correct understanding of the Dutch intervention in Britain in 1688–89, and from then also in Ireland down to late 1691, involves seeing the episode not just as a strategic strike by the United Provinces at the outset of a great European war, designed to remove James II or break his authority and turn Britain round against France so as to help prevent French hegemony in Europe, but also as a political coup designed to strengthen Parliament and the Protestant interest as a means of permanently precluding any likelihood of a resumption of Anglo-French collaboration against the United Provinces.

To correctly grasp the nature of the Dutch intervention in Britain and Ireland it is necessary to get away from the idea that the stadholder was the sole author of the enterprise. In reality, the power of the stadholders in the Dutch Republic was, as Kossmann showed in the preceding chapter, rather limited. It was, for example, totally out of the question for a Dutch stadholder to send the cream of the Dutch army and navy to Britain in November 1688, or at any other time, solely on his own initiative. An expedition on the scale of the Dutch invasion of Britain in November 1688 – the operation involved something like four times as many ships as the Spanish invasion armada of 1588[18] – required not only a good deal of extraordinary recruiting of troops and seamen, and an immense amount of money, but the active collaboration of the Amsterdam burgomasters, the States of Holland, the States General and the admiralty colleges which functioned under the control of the States General. The regents who were the members of these institutions joined forces with William III to intervene in Britain in the autumn of 1688 essentially because they had become convinced that their states, their commerce and their shipping were being gravely threatened by Louis XIV in collusion, to a greater or lesser degree, with the English crown. It may be true that William III to some extent cynically exploited the traumatic memories of the Anglo-French attack on the Dutch Republic which had overrun half the country and paralysed its trade and shipping in 1672. But the fact remains that the Dutch regents were too powerfully under the influence of those painful memories to wish to take the risk of waiting to see if their fears were exaggerated or not. In any case, the feeling was, by the summer of 1688, that the Dutch had to fight France if they were to preserve their trade and shipping in the face of Louis's new guerre de commerce as well as an acceptable balance of power in Europe, and much the best way to counter French power in the context of 1688 was to overthrow James II and turn England round against France. Consequently, the States of Holland, in secret session, took the momentous decision to invade.[19]

However, there was little point in intervening in Britain in an exclusively military and naval capacity. There would have been no sense in taking the enormous risks involved in sending such a large force, with all the best regiments of the Dutch army, some 6000 horses (which alone required around 90 ships) and a great mass of artillery, and at such a late and stormy season in the year, had there not been a very real prospect of being able to mobilise and exploit the deep ideological split in British society: of breaking James II's 'absolute macht' and establishing a new political framework in England. Thus, from the very outset, the Dutch regents and stadholder had a definite interest in introducing something approximating to their ideological model – parliamentary control plus toleration – into Britain. For only through the triumph of Whig constitutional principles was there any likelihood that an Anglo-Dutch alliance against Louis XIV and his jacobite allies could be made enduring and secure. Nor, indeed, without continually stressing the constitutionality of his direction of affairs in England, Scotland

and Ireland, could William III retain the confidence and trust of the Holland regents which was absolutely indispensable to him if his standing in the United Provinces was to remain intact and his European strategy was to succeed.[20]

The constitutional promises embodied in William III's *Declaration* of October 1688 cannot, therefore, simply be dismissed as a short-term tactical ploy. The prince's undertaking in his publicity to restore the 'Liberties' of England and Scotland to their full extent through his cooperation with Parliament, and then to uphold and defend them was, on the contrary, an essential part of the logic of the Dutch intervention in Britain and Ireland in the years 1688–91 and a defining, not an incidental, feature of the Glorious Revolution. In this way it came about that the Whig interpretation of the revolution, though wrong in so many respects, was correct in its final conclusion that the Glorious Revolution was the great and decisive turning point in the making of the British parliamentary system.

5 The United States Constitution and its Roots in British Political Thought and Tradition
Colin Bonwick

Americans, like the British, think they are exceptional. They were the first rebels to succeed against a mighty empire since the United Provinces achieved their independence from Spain; in that and other respects the United States was a self-created nation which stood out in sharp contrast to contemporary anciens régimes that included Britain as well as France and the multitude of other European states. Like the British, they applaud their own constitution and consider it distinctively American and thus unique. And so, in many important respects, it is. Yet it is also clear that the state constitutions as well as the United States Constitution (which were all drafted during the revolutionary era and must be taken together) owe much to the experiences of other countries – and especially to the British constitutionalism from which Americans were escaping.

In many ways, of course, American society after independence was different from Britain. It developed principles, institutions and practices that diverged markedly from contemporary British behaviour. Prescriptive authority, monarchy and parliamentary sovereignty were replaced by popular sovereignty, republicanism, and written constitutions drafted by specially elected conventions and then ratified by the people. The United States also constructed a federal structure within which the states and federal governments divided power between their respective lawful spheres. But the differences should not be exaggerated, for there were limits to American exceptionalism. The United States was geographically and politically an unusually extended society, even in 1776, but its structural complexity was not completely unique. Britain has long been a society of three nations, and four if Ireland can be included; it is now part of a wider union. Furthermore, Britain has become in many ways a crowned republic, and there are important ways in which the United States has shared experiences with Britain and continental Europe rather than stood apart. Thus American success in developing an extended and complex community within an Anglo-American tradition is potentially of great utility to modern European analysts.

The transatlantic community

In reality the United States at the moment of its foundation was both American and a member of a transatlantic community. By the middle of the eighteenth century the Atlantic Ocean had become a highway uniting Western Europe and North America; Nantucket captains who knew how the Gulf Stream flowed regularly made the crossing in 20–30 days.[1] It drew its white population from all over Western Europe, a point to which the presence of large numbers of Dutch in the Hudson Valley, Germans and Scotch-Irish in Pennsylvania, some Swedes on the Delaware River and Swiss and French Huguenots in the south clearly testifies. Building styles in the early republic and the rhetoric of political analysis confirm the obvious. The 13 original states were simultaneously cultural colonies of continental and offshore Europe but also independent entities.

There was indeed a single intellectual world as well as a common trading system across the eighteenth-century Atlantic. Science and philosophy were universal interests that easily extended into politics. Benjamin Franklin's electrical experiments were admired throughout Europe; his embrace with Voltaire at the French Academy in 1778 was a symbolic high point of the Enlightenment. Thomas Jefferson vigorously contested the Comte de Buffon's thesis that American animals were necessarily degenerate versions of their European counterparts, and David Rittenhouse in Philadelphia and other Americans elsewhere joined European astronomers in following the transit of Venus in 1769, while Jonathan Edwards, New England's greatest theologian, attached John Locke's psychology and Isaac Newton's mechanics to John Calvin's predestinarianism as he developed his own theology. By comparison with China, the Islamic empires and the native American societies being dispossessed by Euro-American expansion, Britain and the United States were still at the time of separation members of a single political family. Their differences were those to be expected among nephews, nieces and cousins, not those to be expected between strangers and foreigners. The United States was indeed an intellectual child of Europe.

Within this broad cultural framework, American cultural ties were naturally strongest with Britain. The colonists were patriotic members of the British Empire until the final crisis which precipitated independence, had much day-to-day experience of British political practices (not all of it unhappy), and sent men to fight in every British war in the western hemisphere. There was an extensive network of correspondence and a steady flow of people in both directions; Franklin before the war and John Adams afterwards were only two of many Americans who discussed politics with British friends. In particular there was an extensive literature on all subjects.

Within this literary corpus, Americans were especially familiar with British historical writing and political analysis and the major commentaries on English law; no wonder Thomas Jefferson lauded Francis Bacon, Sir Isaac Newton and John Locke as his intellectual heroes.

Ideology and experience

The United States inherited a network of British structures, principles, and experiences. Superficially, the mainstream of British political values should have been attractive to such loyal members of the empire. To some extent it was, but the experience went sour and there were other more attractive alternatives.

One orthodox thesis was wholly inappropriate for American circumstances from 1776 onwards. Edmund Burke insisted that in reality the passage of time created a right to exercise power. In his view, prescription 'through long usage, mellows into legality governments that were violent in the commencement', and he argued that the British Constitution was the best example of right established by custom since it was 'a prescriptive constitution . . . whose sole authority is that it has existed time out of mind'.[2] Ironically, such a principle scarcely matched the reigning doctrine of the eighteenth-century British Constitution which had only developed in its current form since the Glorious Revolution of 1688–89 before being expounded by Sir William Blackstone 70 or so years later. Nor was the working constitution an entirely satisfactory model for Americans. Far from being written or codified, it was an agglomeration of common law and custom, statute law (including major claims of rights such as the Bill of Rights and Habeas Corpus Act), associated decisions of the courts of law, and above all the institutions of government such as the crown and Parliament, together with numerous conventions which made it operational and the practices by which it adjusted to changing circumstances. These elements were so intermixed that no line was visible between the constitution and normal legislation.

Nevertheless, its central principles were clear. At its heart lay the doctrine of parliamentary sovereignty. Blackstone insisted that Parliament possessed 'uncontrollable authority', was the locus of 'absolute despotic power' and 'could do everything that is not naturally impossible'. Such absolute power was potentially dangerous, but he insisted that the balance between legislature (Parliament), executive (crown) and judiciary functioned as a system of reciprocal checks which prevented each from exceeding its proper powers. Parliament included the balanced estates of monarchy (the crown), aristocracy (the Lords) and democracy (the Commons); within this balance the Lords interceded between king and Commons, thus preventing the crown and people from encroaching on each other's rights. This constitutional balance among its components comprised its true excellence. In a superficial sense Blackstone's system formed, as Montesquieu argued, a complete separation of the executive, legislature and judiciary. In reality, the legislature and executive were anything but separate; the balance was one of interdependent rather than separated parts.[3] Important steps had been taken towards constitutional monarchy and the supremacy of Parliament, but the executive and legislature remained tightly bonded together. By the 1720s ministers of the crown had established control over the House of Commons, and a prime minister's political authority was judged by his ability to command a majority; if he lost it, as Lord North realised he would at the end of the American Revolutionary War in 1783, he was obliged to resign. His instrument was not the will of the electorate, for elections generally followed rather than preceded changes of administration, but 'influence' – or 'corruption' if that term is preferred, as it was by many contemporaries.

Blackstonian principles gave great comfort to orthodox Englishmen but far less to Americans. Fortunately, there were other sources of political principles, including some which literally could be traced back to antiquity. Much American public thought was rooted in the record of the ancient classical world, which was second only to the Bible in their minds. The colonial sense of admirable characteristics was fuelled by the traditional Roman virtues of 'restraint, temperance, fortitude, dignity and independence'.[4] Revolutionary leaders also deeply admired the Greek city-states and especially the Roman republic as models of political organisation, though they were alarmed by the internal decay which they believed was the prime cause of their decline. Thus classical writers such as Aristotle, Polybius and Cicero joined continental writers like Grotius, Burlamaqui, Vattel and Montesquieu as well as British writers as political mentors; similarly, as J.G.A. Pocock has demonstrated, there was an attenuated thread which connected American revolutionary debates to those of Renaissance Florence.[5] Through these writers came a republican tradition that attached great value to social organisation and government as necessary for good citizenship and fulfilment. It also stressed the value of virtue and the duty of placing public welfare ahead of private interest as essential preconditions of republican society, and functioned as a counterweight to the individualist aspects of Locke's philosophy.

Several traditions can be traced back to seventeenth-century England. One which is often neglected is the puritanism that migrated to New England at the moment of its foundation. Two features stand out. The first is the sense of 'calling' which, like republicanism, argued that members of society were ethically obliged to place public welfare and duty before private interest; the second was the organisational structure of gathered Churches which provided a model for political compact and government. Not that it was a uniquely English tradition. Some of the earliest puritan migrants had lived as exiles in Leiden before crossing the Atlantic, and the Dutch contribution to American intellectual culture was substantial. In particular, the Hudson Valley Dutch devised systems of arbitration between landlords and tenants, attached great importance to general literacy and ensured that the Dutch Reformed Church received ministers educated at Leiden or Groningen. But striding across the philosophical landscape was John Locke, who bridged the gaps between orthodoxy and heterodoxy. Grounding his political analysis on natural law and reason and natural rights, he believed that men were obliged by nature to live in society. He insisted that all men were servants of God and had a duty to preserve their fellow men as well as themselves and in order to preserve themselves. To achieve this they entered into a social compact to protect their lives, liberty and property (construed in the broadest sense). Thus natural law and the associated concept of natural rights anticipated the concept of the rights of citizens against government; even Blackstone conceded John Locke's point that the people ultimately retained supreme authority, though he insisted that it was so far removed from current political administration as to lead to the dissolution of government and positive law if the right were to be exercised.

Of all the political traditions, probably the greatest influence on American revolutionary thinking was exercised by a version of the British Constitution known as the 'ancient' or 'anglo-saxon' constitution. It was promoted by a small group of British radicals known as 'real whigs' or 'commonwealth-men', and rested on the myth that a pure anglo-saxon constitution based on the principle of representation had been destroyed by the Norman Conquest. After numerous vicissitudes the Glorious Revolution had marked a renaissance of anglo-saxon principles and the triumph of English liberty. But, the radicals sadly believed, the opportunity it presented had been largely missed. There had been considerable backsliding since 1689, and they especially deplored the corruption by which eighteenth-century governments controlled the House of Commons. Instead they hoped to restore the contemporary constitution to the 'genuine spirit and purity' of the ancient constitution and doggedly defended its fundamental principles, especially liberty. Two of their most influential publicists, John Trenchard and Thomas Gordon, authors of *Cato's Letters* published in 1721–22, argued that liberty was inalienable and 'the Parent of all the Virtues', but insisted that it could not exist without equality. Government was a trust, and its duty was to promote the general welfare.[6] A second central principle of the 'pure' constitution was that all authority derived from the people. James Burgh, writing just before the revolution, explicitly challenged Blackstone's theory of sovereignty by insisting on the sovereignty of the people who, he argued, were superior to government and possessed the authority to remodel it if they wished. In his view, and that of other radicals, 'all lawful authority, legislative, and executive, originates from the people. Power in the people is like light in the sun, native, original, inherent and unlimited by any human. In governors, it may be compared to the reflected light of the moon.'[7] Radicals went on to insist that the separation of powers among legislature, executive and judiciary should be genuine rather than nominal, but the heart of their idea lay in its system of representation. Two things were essential: electors should be capable of exercising genuinely independent political judgement, and Parliaments should refresh their mandate yearly. What radicals feared particularly was uncontrolled power, especially executive power. It followed that the legislature should be free from the corrupting dominance of the executive.[8] Contemporaries generally dismissed their proposals as eccentric at best and dangerous at worst, but most later became law.

Much of this radical literature was widely available in pre-revolutionary America. Tracts by Joseph Priestley, Richard Price, John Cartwright and others were reprinted in the colonies, as was Catharine Macaulay's 'republican' *History of England*. Above all, *Cato's Letters*, which was widely popular for many years, and Burgh's *Political Disquisitions*, whose subscribers included George Washington, John Adams, John Dickinson and Thomas Jefferson when it was reprinted in Philadelphia in 1775, served as influential primers for interpreting events and constructing governments.[9]

Lastly, several representatives of the Scottish Enlightenment exercised a powerful influence on theories of human behaviour which underpinned the political structures erected during the revolutionary era. Thus Thomas Jefferson accepted Francis Hutcheson's argument that men possessed an innate moral sense and in that sense were originally equal. Alexander Hamilton was impressed by David Hume's advice that when constructing governments and fixing limiting constitutional controls it was prudent to consider men as knaves and govern them in the public interest by harnessing their private ambitions and avarice. Hume went on to formulate a theory of interest group behaviour which James Madison developed as the basis of *The Federalist 10*, one of the most penetrating analyses of American politics ever written. Nevertheless, the Scots philosophers denied that men were wholly self-interested. As the republicans argued from different grounds, there were some who were virtuous, and some who were capable of the highest levels of disinterested conduct; these were the men who ought to be selected to govern. And although Adam Smith's market economy thesis ruled much nineteenth-century economic thinking, John Adams used Smith's theory of moral sentiments to develop his own theory of fame as a psychological motivating force.

What is striking is that all these theories of human nature and political behaviour are visible at one point or another in the process of forming new governments in the United States. But the founders did not confine themselves to abstract political theories.

Throughout the process of forming new governments, political ideas were interwoven with the record of actual experience in America and elsewhere. Ideology established general principles and values, and immediate and past experience suggested programmes, strategies and institutions through which they could be implemented. Thus John Dickinson argued at the Constitutional Convention, 'Experience must be our only guide. Reason may mislead us.'[10] Greece and Rome provided a great deal of material, but so did more recent experience. Richard Bland of Virginia declared in 1766 that 'the States of the United Netherlands are instances in the Annals of Europe of the glorious actions a petty People . . . can perform when united in the Cause of Liberty'.[11] During the debates at Philadelphia and in the ratifying conventions, delegates referred more frequently to the United Provinces than to any other continental government. As James Madison, the principal Father of the United States Constitution, prepared for the convention, he worked his way through two trunkfuls of material on earlier and contemporary confederacies, including the Swiss Confederation (which he did not regard as a single commonwealth) and the Dutch Republic. Here he noted divisions of function and authority between the States General and the provinces which anticipated and strengthened to a degree the division between federal and states' authority in the American Constitution, and the apparent security of the other provinces in spite of the dominance of Holland. However, in common with the other delegates he was dismayed by the weakness of the confederation and the apparent impossibility of amending it, perhaps because they misunderstood it.[12] Even if their belief in the weakness of the confederation was exaggerated, however, their argument remained powerful in the circumstances of the convention.

But of course the lessons learned from their experience as British colonies were central. In many ways colonial government mimicked English practice but in a different key. In spite of significant variations from colony to colony a clear general pattern emerged. By the middle of the eighteenth century a royal governor appointed or approved by the crown headed the executive, there was a two-house legislature (except in Pennsylvania) and a judiciary; beneath them a network of counties and townships controlled their own local affairs. Common law principles were adapted to local requirements. But colonial government worked differently from the British system because the balance between executive and legislature was different. In Britain the government of the day controlled the House of Commons and the arrangement worked well because both were populated by members of the landed aristocracy. In the colonies, the legislatures were responsible to the local community who elected them, but governors were responsible to Westminster; it was a recipe for conflict when the system came under pressure.

Yet in some respects the American colonists became more English than the English. Much of their rhetoric was couched in terms of British constitutionalism. Thus the Massachusetts House of Representatives insisted that 'the constitution of Great Britain is the common right of all British subjects', and the Stamp Act Congress of 1765 had declared, 'That it is inseparably essential to the freedom of a people, and the undoubted rights of Englishmen, that no taxes should be imposed on them, but with their own consent, given personally or by their representatives.'[13] Successive British governments denied that the principles of the Glorious Revolution applied to the colonies, but the Americans insisted that they did; and during the eighteenth century they developed on this foundation a constitutional tradition of resistance to arbitrary executive power.[14] Three colonies operated under royal charters whose authority came to be interpreted in two ways. To the British government they were instruments of government and grants of privilege comparable to commercial charters that could be rescinded at will. In the course of time the Americans came to regard them as statements of 'rights' which applied to every colony and could not be unilaterally withdrawn. Instead they became proto-constitutions which set out their right to representative and local self-government and controlled the actions of governments which operated under them.

This sense that charters enshrined major principles became a precedent for the constitutions drafted two years later. Nor was this surprising, since elements of the common law had been transported into the colonies from the beginning. Much concerned land tenure, inheritance rules, criminal law and court procedure, so that Thomas Jefferson in Williamsburg read Bracton and *Coke on Littleton* just as English students did in London.[15] But since they also covered public matters, common law rights were frequently claimed against the crown in times of crisis, and court procedures were used to frustrate royal governors. Nor was the common law tradition lost after independence, for John Dickinson, John Rutledge and the cousins Charles and Charles Cotesworth Pinckney were among several leading delegates to the Constitutional Convention who had read law at the Inns of Court.

Beginning in 1765 the Anglo-American crisis increasingly focused on the nature of sovereignty. The Americans vigorously rejected the Blackstonian principle of parliamentary sovereignty as expressed in the Declaratory Act of 1766 and denied Parliament's claim to legislate for their internal affairs. Nevertheless, they constantly sought to devise an alternative relationship between themselves, the crown and Parliament within the framework of the British Empire. Thus Thomas Jefferson, James Wilson and others constructed possible systems on the eve of war which anticipated in important respects the concept of dominion status of the twentieth century; and so, for that matter, did their friends in England. The experience later helped them to devise a federal system in a complex society; for although the independent states repudiated some features of the British model, they generally remained within the British constitutional tradition in the broadest sense.

As the colonies moved still closer to rebellion then independence, American alarm over another development had a profound effect on their view of government. In dealing with successive British governments the colonists became convinced that a fundamental clash between power (that is, the compulsive dominion of some men over others) on the one hand and liberty on the other underlay every political conflict, including the one in which they were currently engaged.[16] They conceded the need for energy in government – which was essential if citizens were to enjoy their liberty and governments were to fulfil the obligations expected of them, as the defence of independence clearly demonstrated – but became increasingly fearful of expanding and excessive government power. For, as James Madison, the principal architect of the US Constitution, later remarked, 'The essence of government is power; and power lodged as it must be in human hands, will ever be liable to abuse', and as John Adams, 'Atlas of Independence' and second president, perceptively commented, 'Power always sincerely, conscientiously, de tres bon Foi, believes itself Right. Power always thinks it has a great Soul, and vast Views, beyond the comprehension of the weak; and that it is doing God Service, when it is violating all his Laws.'[17] Such opinions were especially pervasive as the Anglo-American crisis deepened, for Americans stood in the same relation to the politics of the British court and government as did the opposition writers. Like their British friends, they wished to return to the purity of the putative ancient constitution; as a North Carolina delegate to the Continental Congress insisted in 1776, 'I am well assured that the British constitution in its purity (for what is at present styled the British constitution is an apostate), was a system that approached as near to perfection as any could within the compass of human abilities.'[18]

American constitutions

The American revolution created a republic whose success depended on selective, not total, emancipation from British political culture. The first state constitutions which, together with the United States Constitution of 1787 formed the new regime, had strong roots in British custom, tradition, principles and practice. Many English constitutional principles were translated, adapted in light of experience, and incorporated into American usage; some came from orthodox English sources, others from the alternative constitutional principles of radical 'commonwealthmen' or 'real whigs' which were often a more attractive paradigm. The same was true of the US Constitution: even the allocation of authority between Congress and the states was essentially a restatement in different terms of the problem the colonists had attempted to resolve within the empire.[19]

The process of development began contemporaneously with the bid for independence in 1776. Each state drafted its own constitution, but though all were confident of the central principles they wished to implement they were unsure exactly how to do it. There was agreement over fundamental principles such as republicanism, popular rather than parliamentary sovereignty, and separation of powers, but a proposal that the Continental Congress should compose a uniform model constitution failed to attract support in 1775, and thereafter each state applied the general principles in its own particular manner. In that respect the state constitutions were both the culmination of colonial ideas on government and the foundation of a national constitutionalism which was articulated first through the Articles of Confederation (ratified in 1781), then through the United States Constitution of 1787.

The process of writing constitutions and the relations between the legislatures and executives demonstrates the states' uncertainty in departing from the parliamentary model. Thus the first New Hampshire Constitution consisted of a small number of general principles, the Virginia Constitution required the governor to be elected by the legislature, and the Pennsylvania Convention conducted normal government business, whereas it was the other way round in South Carolina. Only when Massachusetts Bay got round to electing a special convention whose sole duty consisted of drafting a constitution which included a Declaration of Rights and articulated the separation of powers and the independent election of the governor, and then sent it to the townships for ratification, did a fully distinctive American system emerge.

One of the most misleading contrasts between British and American practice is the apparently unbridgeable distinction between the unwritten and uncodified constitution in Britain and the written state and federal constitutions in the United States. Americans certainly rejected the Blackstonian proposition that there was no distinction between a constitution and a system of law, and William Paley's argument (made later) that the terms 'constitutional' and 'unconstitutional' meant only 'legal' and 'illegal'.[20] Instead, they rested on the alternative principle that there was a controlling higher 'natural' law whose origins could be traced back to the mediaeval English writers Henry de Bracton and Sir John Fortescue and beyond into the classical world.[21] It was also implicit in the doctrine of the ancient constitution and was considered inherent in the charters of those colonies which had possessed them, and the common law as they believed it applied to them, and had been carried forward in the eighteenth-century common-wealthman tradition. It was thus firmly rooted in English thought albeit hidden behind the reigning doctrine, even if some of the quotations during the argument with Britain were drawn from Grotius and Pufendorf. What the states did was formalise uncodified traditional principles into a written code and structure.

Similarly, Blackstone's doctrine of parliamentary sovereignty was overturned by the doctrine of popular sovereignty which underpins the federal constitution and state constitutions alike. The American principle that the people are the exclusive source of all legitimate authority was articulated with especial clarity in the Virginia Declaration of Rights of 1776. It set out four central principles:

> That all men are by nature free and independent and have certain inherent rights . . . That all power is vested in, and consequently derived from, the people; that magistrates [that is, all elected and appointed government officials] are their trustees and servants, and at all times amenable to them. That government is, or ought to be instituted for the common benefit, protection, and security of the people, nation, or community.[22]

Thus the states derived their lawful authority from the sovereignty of their own citizens, not from Congress or the nation at large.

The logic of popular sovereignty also required a social contract among the people to authorise government. There were several sources for this, some religious, some secular. Many of those who shared the drafting of constitutions were practising lawyers who naturally thought in terms of specific contracts. There was a long-standing Puritan tradition of a covenanted people, and the Calvinist doctrine of compact as a basis of Church organisation was easily extended to secular institutions. But above all there were the republican tradition of duty and the Lockean theory of compact, which appeared in a modified form in the state constitutions as well as the

Declaration of Independence, with the vital distinction that whereas Locke articulated a compact between the people on one side and government on the other, the American compact was among the people to form a government that remained subordinate to their ultimate sovereignty where Locke's government was subject only to higher law.

It took some time to work out the separation of powers, especially since the English balance of estates was not fully compatible with American circumstances. But by 1780 the states had formulated a new schema whereby all three components of government were responsible to the people through the medium of their constitutions: in New York and Massachusetts the governors as well as the legislature were elected. An attempt was made to construct a system which assumed that republican citizens were committed to putting the public welfare ahead of private interest, but just to make sure, the constitutions began to install checks and balances as safety devices in case the people failed to conform to this ideal republican model.

In the event independent Americans followed British constitutional procedure by experimenting, adapting and altering their constitutions under the pressure of circumstances while at the same time trying to remain loyal to philosophic principle. Much overlap remained. Common law was one Blackstonian principle that continued to find favour in the states. Similarly, many of the 'rights and liberties of the subject' set out in the English Bill of Rights in 1689 reappeared a century later in the United States Constitution and its accompanying Bill of Rights: the right of petition, prohibition of cruel and excessive punishment, frequent meetings of the legislature, freedom of debate, and the exclusive right of the legislature to raise money and authorise a standing army, for example.[23]

The development of an effective national government was a much slower process. For six years after 1775, Congress functioned essentially as a committee of state ambassadors, though it acquired significant powers (notably those required to prosecute the war) and established limited authority in practice by convention and acquiescence. The first national constitution, the Articles of Confederation of 1781, explicitly acknowledged the sovereignty of the states, and permitted Congress to exercise only those limited powers delegated by them. In particular it was obliged to go to the states for revenue and could implement its decisions only by acting on them rather than directly on the people. The experience of such very limited central government was unhappy, and the 1780s are often described as the 'Critical Period'; only in 1789, when the US Constitution came into operation, did the federal government possess many powers of its own.

The Constitutional Convention, meeting at Philadelphia in 1787, sought to remedy these deficiencies by creating a stable, long-lasting government which would respect the legitimate rights of the states as well as protect the liberties of its citizens and advance their interests in matters of general concern. The powers of the new government to deal with issues of national importance were augmented, and those of the states curtailed, but the constitution erected a union, not a consolidated government.[24] The republican principle of popular sovereignty was preserved in the federal government, first by holding special state ratifying conventions before the new constitution could come into effect, and thereafter by requiring elections to the legislature and, at one remove through the electoral college, the president. The constitution was declared to be the supreme law of the nation, but at the same time each state remained subject to the sovereignty of its own citizens through the medium of its own constitution and the agency of its own system of representation. The new constitution curbed excesses in government by defining its authority and limits, dividing power between the central government and the states (whose legislatures necessarily lost authority in matters of national interest), and introducing checks and balances into the relationship between the three branches of the federal government. In order to achieve these goals, as Forrest McDonald has remarked, 'Whatever their political philosophies most (though by no means all) of the delegates sought to pattern the United States Constitution, as closely as circumstances would permit, after the English constitution.'[25]

In some respects the convention followed the examples of British and state practice alike by separating the powers of government. However, there were significant differences. The British system had been a separation of estates as well as functions, and the Senate and electoral college (which was intended to elect the president) were expected to be populated by members of the elite, who were assumed to be wiser and more disinterested than the mass of the people. The division did not work: in practice American political battles have never divided horizontally between one house and another along class lines. Nevertheless, it enabled the convention to solve the very difficult problem created by having states of differing sizes. The creation of a two-house legislature made it possible to settle the conflict of interests between large and populous states and their smaller sisters; to achieve this the states were equally represented in the Senate but seats in the House of Representatives were apportioned by population. Beyond the question of the structure of the legislature, the constitution rejected the British practice of permitting the executive to control the legislature and the faith displayed in Pennsylvania in particular that direct legislative dependence on the electorate would lead to safe government. Instead, the constitution came closer to the 'ancient constitution' of the anglo-saxons by separating the machinery into three independent branches of government but, to be safe, more checks and balances were introduced by incorporating a deliberate overlapping of powers. The president was given a qualified veto but senior appointments required senatorial consent, for example, and the executive was compelled to parlay with Congress in order to get its proposals enacted into law and to secure ratification of treaties it had negotiated. Thus they shared power and the legislature and executive were obliged to collaborate in the administration of public affairs.

The greatest difference from British practice is the division of powers between the states and the central government, as set out in Sections 8, 9 and 10 of Article I of the United States Constitution. The device employed was the distinctively American principle of divided sovereignty: the federal government for its part and the individual states for theirs each exercised supreme authority within their own sphere of legitimate authority as determined by their constitutions, and all remained subordinate to the ultimate sovereignty of the people. Though not spelled out in explicit language, the division had two great advantages. It further separated the functions of government and thus provided additional institutionalised protection for the liberty of the citizen. Second, and more importantly, it resolved the difficult problem of defining the authority of the states (which in many ways remained the primary units of social and political activity) within a federal system. Yet the division was not absolute, and there was some sharing of authority. For example, the states raised the militia, Congress was entitled to establish general rules, and the president could summon them into national service.

In the United States, the solution to the problem of constructing a permanent union out of 13 distinct states was resolved by assigning certain powers to the federal government, including the power to raise taxes and the control of international and inter-state commerce, and permitting it to establish its own courts, but confining it within its own sphere. In essence, the federal government dealt with foreign affairs, including trade, and matters of general concern including western expansion. For many years it was extremely cautious in asserting its jurisdiction, and there was no public support for its expansion.[26]

The remainder were left to the states. Their laws were required to be consistent with the federal constitution, and their officials were obliged to take an oath to uphold it, but they retained the authority they had acquired from their own citizens through the medium of their own constitutions; they did not acquire it from the national government or constitution. One measure of the effective power of the states as political units was that several major matters had to be left to their judgement, notably the extent of the franchise, the treatment of established religion and, tragically, the status of slavery. But what is striking is that even after 1789 the states did most of the day-to-day governing, and impinged far more actively than the federal government on the lives of their citizens. They controlled property law, estate and inheritance law, commerce within their own boundaries, banking and insurance, family and morals law, general criminal and penal laws, public works and construction, education, local government and natural resources.[27] Not until the New Deal programmes of the 1930s, and some scholars would argue the Great Society programmes of the 1960s, did the federal government develop in a systematic manner the powers that it presently exercises.

In reality, the convention provided an American solution to a more complex version of the same problem that had confronted the four countries of the north-west European archipelago. Over time, England had dealt with the existence of four countries by conquering then digesting Wales during the Middle Ages, and thereafter entering first into a union of crowns with Scotland in 1603 and a century later into a parliamentary union, though at the expense of making important concessions. Indeed, the union with Scotland demonstrated that the doctrine of absolute parliamentary sovereignty was nonsense since it failed to conform to actual political and constitutional behaviour; whatever might happen in the following century, there were Scottish institutions that were outside the Westminster Parliament's effective control. The relationship with Ireland was not satisfactorily resolved.

Britain and the United States move closer

Many features that apparently distinguish American from British constitutional ideas were and have remained closer to each other in actuality than seems to be the case at first sight. Only the American institution of a convention whose sole function is to draft a written constitution that can be placed before the electorate for their approval (or not) has no British counterpart. The contrast between American written constitutions which allegedly remain constant in meaning and character, while the uncodified British Constitution constantly adjusts and adapts itself to changing circumstances, is misconceived. Increasingly the central pillars of the British Constitution have become codified, and a great superstructure of interpretation has been erected over the US Constitution of 1787.

During the nineteenth century Britain began to reform itself. Slowly the radical programmes were enacted and the British franchise moved closer to that of revolutionary America. Some eighteenth-century writers had described the House of Commons as the 'republican' element in Parliament, and the point was picked up by Walter Bagehot. Writing in the 1860s, he was at pains to point to certain similarities between British and American practice. In his view the apparent distinctions between the explicit republicanism of the United States and the ostensible monarchism of Britain were misleading; in England, he declared, 'a Republic has insinuated itself beneath the folds of monarchy'.[28] During the twentieth century the British Constitution has become increasingly, if informally, codified, and has even developed a form of the doctrine of judicial review which had quickly become such a major component of American constitutionalism.

In the opposite direction, it was natural to adapt British constitutional principles and practices to American needs, even if some had to be jettisoned and new ones introduced. The most long-lived element was the common law. Blackstone's doctrine of parliamentary sovereignty was discarded, but his explication of the common law remained profoundly influential in state legal practice. For the first century after independence his *Commentaries* were often reprinted in American editions and were regarded as the basis of legal principles and the 'bible' of American lawyers. Judge Tapping Reeve set out the essence of Blackstone when lecturing at the first American law school, and thus disseminated his principles throughout the new western states.[29] Common law was incorporated into the legal systems of the original thirteen states and every state thereafter except Louisiana, which decided to use the Napoleonic code (although, in spite of the expectations of many lawyers and politicians that it would form part of the federal law of crimes after 1789, it fell out of national use at the beginning of the nineteenth century). In the course of time the original mediaeval system was drastically adapted to changing American circumstances, but according to Richard B. Morris the 1285 statute De Donis Conditionalibus still applied in Illinois, Colorado and Arkansas as late as 1927.[30]

Nor did the US Constitution stand still. From the moment it was instituted it accreted the customs, practices and conventions that were essential if it was to work in practice. This was especially evident in the case of the executive, and in this respect as well as during the War of Independence, George Washington played a literally vital part in establishing the country. Thus Article II of the constitution clearly states that senior federal officials must be confirmed in office by the Senate, but is silent on their dismissal. Washington quickly claimed the exclusive right of dismissal on his own authority, and similarly he asserted the exclusive right to conduct foreign policy, even though Congress undoubtedly possessed the exclusive right to declare war, and treaties required the consent of two-thirds of the Senate present. Quasi-constitutional institutions such as the president's Cabinet and political parties quickly emerged even though they were unmentioned in the constitution and, in the case of parties, generally regarded with abhorrence.

But above all, two major conventions developed that gave the constitution flexibility and the capacity to adapt to changing circumstances and values. The first emerged in 1791 from Secretary of Treasury Alexander Hamilton's need to find constitutional authority to charter a bank, since the power to do so was not explicitly listed in Article I, Section 8: it was the doctrine of implied powers; that is to say, the principle that the constitution need not be construed literally or strictly, but can be interpreted broadly so as to permit the federal government to choose its own methods of achieving the legitimate objectives set out in the constitution, provided those instruments are not unconstitutional by virtue of some other section. The second, which developed more slowly, was the doctrine of judicial review. By the time it came into full flower under the enthusiastic direction of Chief Justice John Marshall, the United States Supreme Court had successfully asserted the right to determine the constitutionality of the actions of all branches of both the federal and the state governments, thus ensuring that the US Constitution, as the supreme law of the land which all officials, state as well as federal, are required to uphold, can be uniformly applied throughout the country.

Implementation of these principles varied considerably over time according to current needs and public wishes. Each generation made its own choice, and through the nineteenth century a very limited national government was what the people desired; full development did not occur until the sequence of crises precipitated by the Great Depression of 1929 and the attack on Pearl Harbor in 1941 followed by the fluctuating wishes of an electorate which first preferred activist government during the postwar years and more recently has changed its mind. Overall then, the United States no longer has an eighteenth-century constitution and in some respects has come closer to British practice than might be supposed.

I have not intended to deny that in certain important respects American constitutionalism differs from British principles and practice; elsewhere I have traced the path by which America achieved its independence in this respect, and I would argue that the two chapters are entirely consistent with each other.[31] What I have sought to demonstrate is that much of the ideology underpinning American political behaviour is derived from European – and especially British – experience and debate and is still compatible with it. To repeat an earlier point, American and British practice are members of the same cultural family and therefore have much in common as well as obvious points of difference. One of the things Americans did was to build on their British political heritage. In particular, they broadened it in such a way as to make it more widely usable by adding a federal element to its constitutional principles and, through the medium of the declarations of rights which introduced many state constitutions and the preamble to the Declaration of Independence, reformulating the rights of Englishmen as the general rights of all men. As they did so they were convinced that their actions had universal as well as domestic importance, and hoped their experience would be helpful to Europeans.

6 Proudhon and Anti-jacobin Federalism
Bernard Voyenne

France is held, not without reason, to be the country of the centralised state. More: it has repeatedly sought to impose that model. This urge may have weakened, but without ever being interrupted. According to a widely held opinion, nationalism, or at least a wary defence of national sovereignty, is always disposed to reappear. Whence, for those who share this view, our difficulty in understanding other traditions.

This generalisation, like many others, contains both the true and the false. Certainly, from Philippe-Auguste to the Jacobins and to Napoleon, by way of Richelieu and Louis XIV, the French state persisted in extending its dominance with a remarkable continuity. It is equally true that, under this deep-rooted influence, it is the unitary model which appeals the most spontaneously to my compatriots, to the extent that supporters as well as opponents of the European Union find it hard to conceive how it could do other than assume that familiar form. They want a unitary Europe or none at all. Not to speak of an element of chauvinism, acute or recurrent, of which the French are far from having the monopoly.

Yet the French have also furnished some of the most ardent apostles of Europe from the nineteenth century on, and above all following World War Two. The names of Robert Schuman and Jean Monnet spring to mind. One may say that centralisers had transposed their concept to a larger stage. It is at the same time certain that, behind the classical orientations of French history, the centrifugal tendencies have hardly been less strong than those which opposed them. The two are indeed complementary.

The turbulence of the Gauls, the plots of the great and the peasant revolts, and the recurrent conspiracies of the factions, have never ceased to counter the dominance of political power to the point where they have repeatedly neutralised it. As far as attachment to the principle of sovereignty is concerned, moreover, our British friends, even if they use a different vocabulary, are just as intransigent, if not more so.

To risk oversimplification, if liberalism found it so difficult to take root in France, that is probably because it seldom responded to popular aspirations, contenting itself to satisfy those of the aristocracy and more generally the privileged – whereas in England and America it appealed to a broader middle class. In France it was from the centre that the hopes of liberation came, against local oppression. Remember the profound analyses of Tocqueville, according to which their passion for equality led the French to seek the protection of power, first royal then republican. In the old English colonies, on the contrary, the prevailing love of liberty favoured the development of free association and hostility to all authority from on high, so striking in the United States to this day.

The ideas of Locke, taken up and enriched by Montesquieu, certainly enjoyed great favour in the course of the eighteenth century in France, to the point where the aspiration of a monarchy limited and respectful of civil liberties, after the English model, was shared by almost the whole of the first revolutionary generation. The Cahiers des doléances, prepared at the level of the parish throughout France for the meeting of the Etats-généraux in 1789, almost all demanded self-government, with all citizens equal before the law. In the first phase of the revolution, the members of the Constituent Assembly looked, for examples of liberty, to Britain, the Netherlands, Switzerland and the US: above all to the US, since the events of 1776 and 1787 had impressed them profoundly.[1] At the great rally of delegations from all over France at the Champ de Mars on 14 July 1790, the federal idea of unity in diversity prevailed; and the Girondins, who were until 1792 the leading party in the Assembly, held to that pluralist conception of unity, along with liberty, individualism and respect for local realities. After they had deposed the king in that year, a significant group sought the adoption of a federal constitution inspired by the American example. But the Jacobins saw the federal idea as a form of subversion: when the Girondins' leader, Jacques-Pierre Brissot, cited *The Federalist* of the American Founding Fathers, he was accused of aiming to destroy the 'Republic, one and indivisible',[2] which the Jacobins regarded as the essential achievement of the revolution. Following Jean-Jacques Rousseau's dictum that the social contract 'gives the body politic an absolute power' over all its members, directed by the general will,[3] they opposed the Girondins' philosophy root and branch. It was the Jacobins who secured the more popular support; and their violent campaign against the Girondins led directly to the Terror, which led in turn to Napoleon's authoritarian regime.

It appears that most of the bourgeoisie, on the contrary, even the 'progressives', would have settled for a reform that would guarantee them economic power, with a state limited to ensuring its protection. The priority for the nation was, in their eyes, to guarantee the rights of the citizen, above all the protection of their property, more or less legitimately acquired. For the poor, on the contrary, this nation supposedly conquered by the people should vest in itself the whole of the ancient royal prerogatives, extended if necessary to the ownership of land. They accepted the yoke of the state, provided it would ensure them a modicum of well-being. The republic represented for them the symbolic person of the monarch transferred to the society: that is why it could not be divided. To challenge it was the crime of lese-majesty par excellence: that of federalism, which led to the guillotine for Girondins, royalists or dissidents of all kinds.

The genius of Napoleon was to confiscate, to his own advantage, both the people's need for protection and the new power of the bourgeoisie. The honour of the flag was engaged in foreign wars, internal security restored by uniform laws, fear of disorder exorcised by an omnipresent police. By these means the French accepted the return (attributed henceforth to 'merit') of the forms of royalty, for which they were probably nostalgic after having hated it so much. The owners of property breathed again, the masses were fascinated by the éclat of the regime, the vast majority of the Voltairian intelligentsia traded its conscience for a fistful of privileges. France was once again convinced that, without a strong state, she could not be truly herself.

So the jacobin ideal triumphed on the ruins of its dream. Under the napoleonic rod, the old gallic spirit was brought to heel, the complex network of diversities gave way to a military rigour, and civil liberties had to bow to the superior interest of the country. A whole set of changes inspired by an impeccably geometric spirit transformed the country more profoundly than the revolution had been able to do. The citizen, who had been promised that he would be king, was no more than a cog in an immense machine conceived exclusively to produce power.

The way to modern society lay open. A triumphant class, the bourgeoisie, was ready to manage it. Over against it a separate class was formed, the proletarians – who owned only their plot of land or nothing – forming the body of this leviathan. Since it had ended in the Terror, the individual aspired, in place of unbridled liberty, only to the shelter of a soft absolutism, invisible although everywhere present, oppressive though held to be the sole defence of the weak against the others and against themselves. Thus the jacobin concept of a powerful centralised state became entrenched in the French polity, opposed by only two significant streams of thought: that of the liberals such as Constant and Tocqueville who, like the Girondins, looked to the anglo-saxon model; and an original French variety that was to exert much influence on the workers' movements, based on the ideas of Pierre-Joseph Proudhon.

Proudhon against absolutism

Born under the empire, Proudhon (1809–1865) was, if not the only one to reject the new tyrannies of state and capital, at least the most stubborn and consequent in his rebellion. He was the one, too, to take the measure most lucidly of the adversaries in order never to fall, as he was to write to Marx, into the trap of their errors: 'Let us not make ourselves the leaders of a new intolerance, nor pose as the apostles of a new religion, even if it should be the religion of logic and of reason.'[4]

This proud descendant of a line of peasants and workers was not a 'notable'. He had known poverty and owed almost nothing to the establishment. Even his intellectual attainments, vast though they were, had to be seized from the established education and then enriched in practising the trade of a typographer, thanks to a sort of contraband of culture. It is also relevant to mention his origin in the Franche-Comté: a province alongside Switzerland, eccentric in relation to the French system and jealous of its liberties. We are dealing at the same time with an authentic product of a certain tradition, but also with an exceptional individual who would not let himself be confined within any formula. Even if he had been a writer only, these traits were already far from common.

That said, Proudhon was a son of the Enlightenment, in the line of Locke who had evidently inspired in him this definition: 'Politics is the science of liberty . . . .' But while that was entirely Lockean, the young Proudhon, reacting against the tradition of the jacobin centralised state, went on to aver that 'the government of man by man, under whatever name it be disguised, is oppression'.[5] He was, as we shall see, unlike the marxists, to come later to understand that the removal of oppression would not remove the need for government, and to seek a just balance between liberty and authority. But his first concern was to oppose the jacobin concept of the state. Thus he was a thoroughgoing heir of the great Revolution, but in revolt against what it produced. A libertarian, he struggled to understand how the movement of 1789 could engender the horrors of 1793. As passionate for equality as any enragé, his big problem was to give the lie – well before he knew of it – to the pessimism of Tocqueville's conclusion that, for the French at least, liberty was not compatible with equality.

The axiom to which Proudhon never ceased to adhere is that men would not be free if they were not equal, but that the converse is no less necessary. That led him moreover to his stand against absolutist property – the 'right to use and to abuse' – as defined in the *Code Napoléon*. It was that which established, then maintained through the mechanism of unrestricted interest, the fundamental inequality in the society, with all its consequences. However, and this did not fail to cause him to be accused of contradiction, he refused with equal energy the collectivisation of property to which the revolutionary logic tended to lead, because he lucidly saw in it a no lesser source of tyranny.

Thus, already in his first writing, Proudhon produced, echoing Rousseau but already against him, the formulation: 'Find a state of social equality which is neither communism nor despotism, neither disintegration nor anarchy, but liberty in order and independence in unity.'[6] Note, since we shall return to it, the use of the word 'anarchy' in its usual (banal) sense, whereas Proudhon was soon to claim this label as the one that suited him the least badly – though one should remember its etymological sense: 'no governmentalism'.

This terminological point aside, it is striking to see that the federalism which will become in his last works the indispensable complement of anarchism was already present at least implicitly in his thinking at the outset: present, moreover, in the two complementary forms, political and economic, that will comprise its specificity.

Few authors' works present such continuity, inspired from beginning to end by an intention that is never repudiated. None, in the long history of political thought, so deliberately runs counter to the ideas of both left and right, to go beyond what the author believes to be a false debate. Proudhon's thought comes from nowhere else and intends to lead to somewhere else. That is what justifies its interest and foreshadows its actuality, despite all the subsequent upheavals.

The rule of contract

All the first part of Proudhon's life – some 20 years of research and of sensational interventions in the life of his time – was devoted to struggle against the absolutist form of property sanctified by the bourgeois revolution and the system of government that necessarily stemmed from it. He called in question both the certainties of political economy, still a new discipline, and the dreams of the old utopianism. Polemicising on all fronts, against the liberals or the socialists, the works of this period based his mutualist theory of society on an original analysis of work, exchange and credit. That was notably the case of the two large volumes of *Contradictions économiques,* which provoked the wrath of Marx.[7]

The pivot is the contract, formulation taken again from Rousseau but to arrive at opposite conclusions. According to Proudhon then, once the fundamental inequality between owners and proletarians had been abolished, the individuals and groups would become free to conclude mutual agreements regulating their life together. These would in fact be essentially of an economic nature, because the will to individual power would be excluded by definition. Political institutions, whose purpose is to maintain the supremacy of the privileged, would have no more raison d'être: 'The idea of contract excludes that of government.'[8] It was the workshop that would replace the state, Proudhon continued, taking the word in the all-embracing sense of place of production, in the framework of which each would deal to the best advantage, according to the liberal idea at last rendered effective.

That is the anarchist vision of which Proudhon was the founder: not in the sense of an individualism rejecting any rule other than his own – such as that of a Stirner[9] – but in the radically different acceptance of a social state permitting the human being to develop fully his relations with others, because it would have destroyed the cause of oppression.

If he chose the term 'anarchy', although it evoked almost universal reprobation, it was a gesture of bravado in which he who had become famous for proclaiming 'La proprieté c'est le vol'[10] indulged with such delight. But more profoundly, if one takes this scarecrow-word with the grain of Proudhon's thought, none would better define a truly free society whose members, obeying only themselves, would at the same time respect the same indefeasible right for all. The influence of the Kantian imperatives on the author of *Justice*[11] is undeniable and, certain reservations apart, he himself recognised it.

Struggle for justice

Closely involved in the events of 1848–49, Proudhon rapidly distanced himself, not only from the triumphant reaction but also from his own camp. Solitary, misunderstood even by his comrades in the struggle, he drew the lessons of a defeat whose causes he perceived better than anyone in the book which is without doubt – it was at least the view of Sainte-Beuve – his best from the literary point of view: *Confessions d'un révolutionnaire.*[12] Then, aged 39, this confirmed bachelor got married, even when he had just been put in prison for two extremely violent articles against Louis-Bonaparte, who was on his way to becoming emperor.

From his relatively easygoing gaol, the incorrigible controversialist continued to direct his journals and published a new book, the *Idée générale de la Révolution au XIXème siècle*,[13] in which, as the title indicates, he condensed all his preceding views while giving them a particularly aggressive form. The revolution, for him, had nothing to do with epiphenomena such as violence in the street or the replacement of one holder of authority by another: it consists in abolishing all power of man over man, or it is nothing. In a series of vengeful reproaches, Proudhon pushed to an extreme his anarchist doctrine, affirming that all governments, whatever their label, were merely the same despotic oppression. He continued to oppose to this the vision of a society governed only by the relations of exchange and mutual benefit.

Paradoxical as always, however, the same man profited from his enforced leisure to undertake a vast overview of political history and, in particular, of the different constitutions, present or past. Thus a period of reflection began which led him to review in the course of a few years a number of his ideas, to give them a greater scope. This led, under the influence of both an inner compulsion and fortuitous circumstances, to the great philosophical treatise: *De la Justice dans la Révolution et dans l'Église.*[14]

The purpose of this work of nearly 2000 pages, the most ambitious that he had written, was to serve for the education of the people by ordering around a central theme the whole range of questions posed by the social transformation, including those that Proudhon had so far left to one side. The two poles of the dialectic equality–liberty, more than ever at the heart of his thinking, were brought together, though not merged, in the scales of justice. Since his first work, Proudhon had called it 'the central axis that governs societies'.[15] Immanent in man and transcending history, it is the only authority that human dignity can accept, the unique sovereignty that cannot be oppressive because it is that of justice.

The state

In a special study in the fourth volume of *Justice*, Proudhon showed interest for the first time in the state, not now in a negative manner but as a subject in itself. From now on he accorded it a place, albeit subordinate, provided that its function was to guarantee justice. Thus the conditions must be strictly defined. This evolution, which began with the studies undertaken during the years in prison, took place in the course of the exile in Belgium which was imposed on him by the threat of a new conviction.

Matured, perhaps wiser, certainly more au fait with the upheavals that were in the course of transforming Europe, he who had been the ardent defender of the social and nothing but the social felt more and more concerned with the political. He began to admit, without expressing it in quite that way, that the advent of anarchy by his definition was not for tomorrow. The revision of his earlier ideas, moreover, caused an asymmetry to appear, of which his analysis of the implications of justice made him aware. No more than authority could liberty reign without sharing: it was from the tension between them that the movement of societies proceeded.

Since the 1860s, moreover, while in exile, he had been particularly attentive to the danger for the peace of Europe of the current process of Italian unification in the jacobin mode, with the blessing of Napoleon III; and still more that of Germany which did not fail to follow. These considerations were the fuel for the book *La Guerre et la Paix*,[16] from which

Tolstoy took his title. Nearly simultaneously they gave rise to a series of polemical writings. Almost all concerned the question of nationalities, of which the left had become enthused to the point of making it the sole consolation for their failures.

This innate defender of autonomy certainly held that the right of people to control their own lives could not be contested. Nothing must prevent those who are liberated from oppression from uniting among themselves according to their affinities, on condition that they do not lose by it the most precious good of all, for which they had fought: liberty. But not only does a monolithic unity suppress the liberty of its own citizens in making subjects of them, it also leads fatally to a confrontation between sovereignties, condemned to seek domination in order not to be dominated. That was precisely what was in the course of happening. Prophetically, Proudhon wrote:

> We are marching towards a formation of five or six great empires . . . So there will be in Europe neither rights, nor liberties, nor principles nor morals. So the great war of the six great empires against each other will also begin . . . Europe culpable will be chastised by Europe armed.[17]

Federalism

The facts are there. Even if one may be alarmed about the consequences of some, others are ineluctable and can even be generators of progress. It is not enough to say 'Leave things alone and all will be well', for such conservatism is an impasse. On the one hand, groups of people have a full right to autonomy, that is clear. But, on the other, the march towards unity also corresponds to a normal human aspiration and must therefore find its political form. How to reconcile these two tendencies: that which seeks to save the diversities and that which aspires to make justice reign over the largest possible space? Cultivated for itself, particularism encloses itself in isolation and can become as baneful as the claim to omnipotence. This contradiction must be broken.

It is thus that Proudhon arrived at federalism, around which his reflections had always circled but, for a variety of reasons, had skirted without fully grasping it. As the root tells, federation signifies contract in its widest sense. That was already the idea of 'mutuality' which, complementing the division of labour by the reciprocity of services rendered, would abolish the exploitation of man by man. The same word covers equally the preceding definition of 'anarchy' which, far from exalting disorder, proposed to install a freely consented order. 'Through a simple synonym',

Proudhon wrote, struck by his discovery, 'the whole revolution is given to us, political and economic.'

What in effect differentiated the federalism of Proudhon from the Swiss example – despite his origins in the neighbouring Franche-Comté – is that it goes beyond the political organisation among geographical units, and applies to the whole of the social field. In this perspective, it is *all* the activities that should become progressively federalised to form the 'agricultural-industrial federation', in conformity with the requirements of justice. That federalism proposes much more than to ensure a cohabitation, even a successful one: its ambition is nothing less than to build 'a world fit to live in'.

The same characteristic distinguishes it from the federalism of which Hamilton and his friends were the protagonists, which found its expression in the constitution of the United States. A further difference is no less important. The American problem was in effect to impose a quasi-monarchical unity on the centrifugal resistance of the colonies. That was, moreover, realised only slowly and at the cost of a civil war: a situation partly analogous, apart from the violence, with that of Europe today. But Proudhon's perspective is almost the reverse. For him the liberty of the component parts remains fundamental: they must unite without becoming alienated. In this perspective his position in favour of the South in the War of Secession was striking (just as he took the side of the Sonderbund at the time of the conflict in Switzerland), despite all that could have moved him to a contrary choice. Nobody has shown a greater attachment than he to the anglo-saxon principle of self-government, whose full development he wanted to ensure.

Thus delayed, at least in its full expression, the theory of federalism almost exclusively occupied the last years of his life. It is at the centre of two great works: *Du Principe fédératif et de la nécessité de reconstituer le Parti de la Révolution*[18] – whose title is in itself a programme – and *De la Capacité politique des classes ouvrières*,[19] more specifically devoted to the economic and social aspects. Illness prevented the first of these books from finding a fully satisfactory form, and interrupted the second before completion of the final chapter. Nevertheless, complemented by other texts of the same period, these are the indispensable references for anyone who wishes to be informed about this philosophy.

Proudhon's vision had a powerful impact on a notable part of the workers' movement, in France as in other countries, from the creation of the first International right up to World War One. The trade unions, in particular, organised themselves in the federal manner and inscribed the mutualist principles in their statutes. But after 1917, the bolshevik revolution swept away and systematically persecuted all who in one way or another adhered to the libertarian current.

Reacting against this obfuscation, a 'return to Proudhon' became evident in various milieus from the 1930s on, notably in groups claiming kinship with personalism. It is there too that one finds, in the same period, the strongest opposition to the rise of national socialism and to the Stalinist (or other) marxism that then dominated the greater part of the left.

A number of these proudhonians, and not the least of them, were to be found among the pioneers of the European idea. Without doubt the latter had multiple origins, some of them ancient: in particular the cosmopolitanism of the Enlightenment, the followers of Saint-Simon and most of the socialist schools of the nineteenth century, the pacifism of post-1918. But among those who gave the decisive impulse, while one can rightly cite Churchill, Schuman, Monnet, De Gasperi, Spaak, that of the federalists who played just as active a role is not sufficiently known. A number of them took part, during the 1930s, in the review *L'Ordre Nouveau*, inspired by Arnaud Dandieu and animated by Alexandre Marc, Denis de Rougemont and Robert Aron, to mention only those directly concerned with our subject. After 1945 they were joined by a certain number of trade unionists faithful to the 'Charte d'Amiens' of 1906, non-marxist socialists and elements from diverse components of social catholicism.

Marc was a founder and the first Secretary-General of the European Union of Federalists (EUF), which held its founding congress at Montreux at the end of August 1947 and took the initiative for the 'États généraux de l'Europe' which, along with Winston Churchill's speech of 19 September 1946 at Zurich, was at the origin of the historic Congress of Europe held at The Hague on 7–10 May 1948. From that followed the Council of Europe and the European Movement, soon overtaken by the first step, deliberately supranational, towards European union: the European Coal and Steel Community (ECSC), launched on 9 May 1950. While the ECSC was the fruit of an initiative that was more pragmatic than doctrinal, in whose origins the proudhonians did not participate directly, it none the less conformed with their ideas, as their support for it clearly demonstrated.

Although its successor, the European Union of today, does not satisfy the proudhonian federalists, it is significant that Jacques Delors, who is linked with the Christian personalist group, was so ready to embrace the 'principle of subsidiarity', a term of scholastic origin equivalent to the principe fédératif as Proudhon defined it:

What makes the essence of the federative contract . . . is that in this system the contractors . . . reserve for themselves individually, in forming the pact, more rights, liberty, authority, and property than they give up.[20]

Subsidiarity, even if not properly applied, is now official doctrine of the European Union. It seems, too, that France, even if still far from having abandoned the jacobin centralism that Proudhon abhorred, has been moving towards the decentralisation for which he fought. It may be legitimate to hope that this, combined with the consolidation of liberal political structures in a more anglo-saxon sense, may be moving France towards a federalism in both the proudhonian and the hamiltonian traditions. Ideas are always on the move.

7 Anglo-saxon Influences and the Development of German Democracy after World War Two

Anthony Glees

In his first major speech to the minister-presidents of the Länder in the US zone, delivered on 17 October 1945 only six months after the capitulation of the Third Reich, the most important American in Germany, General Clay, gave a clear account of American aims. Re-reading them, more than 50 years later, it is remarkable how honest they were but, above all, how deep was the commitment to democracy. It was made clear to the western Germans the self-evident truth that Germany did possess a democratic tradition; but that it had not been good enough. Restoration of Weimar was out of the question. Clay emphasised the importance of treating Nazism as an illegal and criminal activity, but that once it had been dealt with appropriately, complete liberal democracy would come quickly. Indeed, at the end of his speech he bluntly stated that democratic elections for local government would be held in January 1946, sooner than the German democratic forces themselves wanted.

Clay declared:

US policy on Germany is firm policy. It may seem bad but it has been made to destroy the war potential of Germany. It does not have as its theme the destruction of the German people. It includes as a primary objective complete de-Nazification which requires not only the removal of Nazis from places of prominence in all parts of German life, but will also provide for the separation from the Nazis of any wealth accumulated as part of Nazi activity. We have made many mandatory arrests. For security reasons the arrestees have been prevented from communicating with their families. This is not the American way and we will shortly permit arrestees to notify their families of their whereabouts.

He continued:

Our policy includes complete demilitarisation . . . concentration of industrial power will be dispersed. On the positive side of the picture, we propose to return to you as quickly as possible the responsibility for self-government. Our policy calls for decentralisation of governmental authority in the Länder units. We propose to start the election of responsible assemblies at the Gemeinde levels in January next year. We understand that a number of you feel this is too soon. However, we know of no other way in which the working of the democratic process can be placed underway in Germany. We propose to return to you a free press and radio at the earliest possible date. You now have a complete freedom of religious worship. We also propose to remove any blocks which we may have placed in the way of liberal educational opportunities. In increasing the governmental authority at the Land level we still believe in the operation of Germany as an economic unity . . . the securing of administrative co-ordination is your task . . . .[1]

At the equivalent British event, a conference held at Detmold on 19 and 20 November 1945, General Templer, an equally impressive figure, made a similar point:

One of our major objects in this country is to develop democracy having due regard to the German character, history and present political development. You are also to be quite clear in your minds that we have no intention of imposing a purely British concept of democracy on Germany. As a matter of fact, the Military Government directive on local government is not a purely British thing but it is common form throughout the whole democratic world. It is no use saying that Germany had an excellent democratic system in the past. That system was not good enough to prevent the seizure of power by anti-democratic forces. A thoroughly democratic system may not be superficially as efficient as an authoritarian one. The fact remains that if it is given time to develop, it produces the spirit from which it is possible to organise the nation for any event and, what is extremely important, to achieve a far greater degree of fundamental political stability.[2]

As we shall see, anglo-saxon policy over the next four years complied to a remarkable extent with these broad aims, progressing through three different paradigms: the punitive, the colonial-constructive and partnership.[3]

From defeat to the Potsdam Conference

Anglo-saxon policy must be set not only in the context of high occupation policy, but in the physical condition of Germany in 1945. The situation facing the Allies in Germany was one of complete and utter chaos. Millions were on the move as refugees, displaced persons uprooted by the Germans and used as slave labour, Germans seeking to escape the control of the Red

Army (and the bolshevik control Goebbels had predicted), war criminals and other leading Nazis trying to escape capture. German civic culture had been virtually destroyed. Millions were without a roof over their heads. People were starving.

From this unpromising starting point, the policies pursued by Germany's victors during 1945–49 constitute perhaps the most important of the processes that formed the Federal Republic. The most significant changes in German political development, both in the West and in the East, were the changes made during the years of occupation by those who had fought against Hitler's Germany, rather than by the Germans themselves. In the West, it was the Americans who did most to shape the Federal Republic; in the East, the Soviet Union constructed its model German state.

It was the western Allies' occupation that made democracy viable. A 'Germanic' form of government, whether of the extreme left or the ultra Conservative right (the centre, still paralysed, quickly took its cue from the Americans), was simply not permitted to take root. It was the occupiers who now defined German interests and framed German affairs, both domestically and externally. This came to an end, with certain exceptions, after a decade. But with the striking exception of the Soviet system, what was created lasted for two generations at the very least.

The first phase of occupation was hallmarked by a punishment paradigm. A punitive and colonial system was imposed on Germany, which employed new legal means to criminalise Hitler's most wicked racist supporters, along with the state they had created. As Noel Annan has made plain, 'democracy in Germany could not be born unless it was delivered with the forceps of de-Nazification'.[4]

Once this was done as well as it could be (even if not well enough), a second phase began. For the west of Germany, this was characterised by constructive occupation, leading to real cooperation and then partnership. The Allies now began to impose democratic political structures – parties and political institutions – on the Germans. What was done was not generally the result of any wholly new invention. West Germany was different from other German states, but it was German and not American, British or French. On the whole, German political and institutional forms were adapted, and filled with western liberal contents. In the West, at any rate, it was, therefore, a veritable re-invention of Germany.[5]

The wartime Allies had different political ideas and competing security interests. What had been Germany was now affected by at least five different external entities. These were the occupation policies of the individual victors in their own zones, and the jointly agreed policy on Germany as a whole, to which must be added a domestic German input that could lead to a political decision only if it enjoyed the support and gained the final approval of the occupying powers, for each victor retained ultimate authority over legislation. Each of these inputs had its own special aspect. Out of them, two new German states were fashioned and German political life assumed a new and very difficult shape.

We thus need to pay regard both to policy agreed between the Allies, as formulated at Potsdam (to which the French were not invited) and at the council or formal meetings of their foreign ministers (in which France did participate) as well as to the individual agendas of the Allied powers. Over and above all of this, we must bear in mind that the two German states were forged out of superpower conflict, against a backdrop fashioned by the fear of nuclear and, after 1953, thermonuclear war. Atom bombs and then hydrogen bombs added huge danger to all differences in policy. These bombs, which were able to crack open the earth's outer mantle, ended up solidifying the political geography of the two parts of Germany. Neither superpower dared interfere with the other. Thus by 1947 the differences in intention between the superpowers and the ensuing Cold War became the determining factor in their respective foreign policies and their policy on Germany.

The Potsdam Conference – appropriately code-named Terminal – was held in what was considered the home town of Prussian militarism (in a mock Tudor palace). It did not lead to a treaty, but to a protocol, a report upon which there was Allied agreement. It ended one sort of German nation and planned for another.

The participants in the conference were Harry Truman, the new American president; Clement Attlee who, just as the conference began, replaced Winston Churchill as the British prime minister; and Joseph Stalin. The conference produced quick agreement on the 'five Ds': demilitarisation, de-Nazification, disarmament, democratisation and decentralisation (the Soviet Union tended to forget the latter two). It was decided that economically Germany was to be treated as a single unit. It was also agreed that the Allied Control Council meeting in Berlin would take unanimous decisions on all matters affecting Germany as a whole, although within their own zones, the military commanders-in-chief had full authority. Finally, the Potsdam agreement established a council of foreign ministers (which was to be joined by the French foreign minister) to meet at regular intervals. It was charged with special duties for the process of making peace in the future, especially with the future German state.

Despite their apparent personal wish to see the deconstruction of German national unity, neither Roosevelt nor Churchill was willing to build this into their national policies on Germany. There was agreement that the power of a central German government needed to be curtailed, given Germany's inherent strengths which would, one day, reappear. But this was not the same as suggesting that Germany be split up into various separate sovereign nations. Indeed, the extent to which Germany's dismemberment was not high policy is surely demonstrated by an examination of all the agreements reached at Potsdam. The dismemberment of the nation itself was never a sixth 'D'.

The Potsdam protocol, signed on 2 August 1945, laid down the basis for the political and economic control of Germany under occupation. In the event, its writ disintegrated within two years. Some German historians have argued that as a consequence the agreement was a work of fiction and that the decision to treat Germany as separate units for the purpose of reparations in effect created two German states. This is not plausible. The underwriting of the existence of a four power Allied High Command in Berlin to coordinate policy in all the zones of Germany as well as the decision that economically Germany was seen as a single unit can be seen as the outcome of a clear intention to retain an element of all-German government.

From Nuremberg towards the founding of the Federal Republic

The first step in the abolition of Hitler's ethnic order was to criminalise those who had directly executed it and tear up the laws that had upheld it. There had been eight and a half million members of the Nazi Party and four million members of associated organisations. The Allies had to set up 545 courts (staffed by 22,000 officials) to process the 3.5 million questionnaires completed by former Nazis.

The effects of the Allied war crimes policy on politics in western Germany (as well as on the rest of the world) should not be underestimated. The effective criminalisation of Nazi party members and sympathisers (even if only on paper) permitted a distinction to be drawn between Nazis and Germans – to the huge advantage of the latter. Not every Nazi had been a war criminal but Nazism itself became illegal. The policy enabled western Germany to be purged to a relatively satisfactory degree. Although only a small proportion were convicted, mostly of minor crimes,[6] the policy allowed West Germany to enter the community of western liberal states far quicker than would otherwise have been possible. And with one or two relatively minor exceptions, 1930s Nazism was successfully excluded from German public affairs. This was a tremendous achievement.

The Nuremberg Tribunal generated 13 separate trials involving 177 people and passed 20 life sentences, 25 death sentences and 35 acquittals. They were charged on one or more of four counts: the common plan or conspiracy, crimes against peace (the planning and waging of aggressive war), war crimes (here defined as shooting prisoners of war), and crimes against humanity (here defined as the persecution of Jews and the destruction and exploitation of occupied territories). As Lord Shawcross, a leading British lawyer at Nuremberg, said many years later:

> Historically, Nuremberg was certainly justified in the sense that it wrote the history of some terrible things in connection with the war and its preparation that would never have been written without such a trial. It was conducted with great fairness. Everybody who was condemned to death had committed murder, not just a single murder, but murder, ordinary murder on a vast scale.[7]

At Potsdam it had been agreed that all members of the Nazi Party who were more than nominal members were to be dismissed, and for the next year and a half almost 1 million Nazi Party members had to resign from the bureaucracy. By the end of 1946 the British had interned 64,000 'dangerous Nazis', the Soviets 67,000, the French 19,000 and the Americans 100,000. In the three western zones to 1950 more than 6 million cases were investigated: 1667 people were classified as major, 23,060 as minor and 150,425 as perpetrators; 1,005,854 as fellow travellers (of whom two-thirds were punished in some way) and 1,213,873 as innocent. In another 4 million cases, amnesties were given for various reasons (including youthfulness).

The colonial-constructive paradigm

Against the background of increasing tension with the Soviet Union (which neither America nor Britain sought, or wanted), the Americans followed by the British decided to address the growing economic problems of western Germany without waiting for the Soviet Union to agree on the form of the new single German state. They set up the bizone in 1947 in order to unite the US and UK zones and thus restore the German economy in the west. To expedite this, an Economic Council was set up, with representatives to be chosen by the Land Parliaments. In 1948 the French zone joined the bizone, forming in effect a trizone. The Economic Council was expanded, a Länder council was set up alongside it, and a German supreme court and central bank were established.

It was America's belief that a new economic order was necessary, not only to lay the foundations for future prosperity, but also to permit western-style democracy to flourish. On 12 March 1947, in an address to Congress, President Truman called for a $400 million economic and military aid package to Greece and Turkey, adding the keynote phrase that 'it must be the policy of the United States to support free peoples who are resisting attempted subjugation by armed minorities or by outside pressures, primarily through economic and financial aid, which is essential to economic stability and orderly political progress'. This was followed on 5 June by the speech of his Secretary of State at Harvard, initiating what became known as Marshall Aid. Its political and economic effects were enormous. They not merely led to the economic regeneration of western Europe and the creation of the European Community, but also confirmed the political division of the continent.

This American policy had a profound impact on the shaping of Germany's future. Western Germans used Marshall Aid first for food and then for modernising their industrial base and building homes. The impact on them of this act of American generosity was enormous; it played a key part in locking West German democracy into the Atlantic relationship and, by helping to produce such prosperity, ultimately proved to the people of Eastern Europe and the Soviet Union that communism could not compete with the liberal western economy.

In order that the three western zones of Germany should be able to participate fully in the Americans' European recovery plan, it was necessary to deal with German hyperinflation. Increasingly, the cigarette had become a unit of currency. It was thus vital to restore real money to western Germany. This was done in a series of four laws, of which the most obvious was the German currency law of June 1948, which gave every individual 40 units of the new money, the Deutsche Mark, or DM; later they were to get another 20. Within ten days all old Reichsmarks had to be handed in and changed at a value of 10:1, although half of this had to be kept in a closed bank account. This huge (and inevitably secret) operation was masterminded by Ludwig Erhard, in charge of the West German end, and the Americans.

The Soviet response was crude: to seek to detach West Berlin from the West. At the beginning of 1948, the Soviets had begun to interfere with transport to West Berlin. Since all land access and all three air corridors went through Soviet controlled territory, it was clear that their power to blockade Berlin was enormous. On 24 June, in an attempt to prevent the transfer of the western Mark into West Berlin, Soviet forces imposed a complete halt on western land traffic to Berlin.

Stalin's aim was plainly to starve the two million inhabitants of West Berlin into surrendering to communism by accepting the eastern Mark. Whilst the Americans had atom bombs as a deterrent, they were, for obvious reasons, of little use in this case; and the advice that General Clay was giving to the American president was that Stalin, too, did not wish to have a nuclear war over West Berlin. The western Allies decided to defeat the Russians not through military force but by a demonstration of their technical superiority.

As a result, Operation Vittles, the airlift of food and fuel, was initiated on 7 July and within a few days 3000 tons were flown in; one day, 13,000 tons of food were transported in 1400 flights to Tempelhof, Gatow and Tegel (British seaplanes even landed on the Havel). There could be no more basic or emotive illustration of the western commitment to the German people than an airlift whose purpose was not military but to keep people alive and to prevent them from being blackmailed. The point that those who had three years previously been the mortal enemies of the West were now treated as its allies escaped no one in the West or the East. The Berliners themselves came out of it with much praise, not least because of their humour ('good that the Russians are providing the blockade and the Americans the airlift, rather than the other way round'); but it should not be forgotten that in the process of making 300,000 flights (and delivering 2 million tons of goods), 39 British and 31 American servicemen gave their lives.

American occupation policy

US policy on Germany in its zone was the dominant policy, thanks to American power. Its original basis was the Joint Chiefs of Staff Document 1067, usually referred to simply as JCS 1067. Henry Morgenthau, Roosevelt's treasury secretary, took the line that in order to punish the Germans, and prevent them from ever again being strong enough to wage aggressive war, it was necessary to de-industrialise and pastoralise Germany and to dismember its national unity. JCS 1067 came to possess the clear mark of Morgenthau. Truman signed it on 14 May 1945. He also continued his predecessor's policy of seeking to cooperate fully with the Russians. General Eisenhower, who was US military governor in Germany until November 1945, also firmly believed in the value of cooperation with the Soviet Union and felt considerable bitterness towards the Germans ('I won't shake hands with a Nazi', he once declared). After his departure, real power was exercised by General Clay, first as deputy governor and then, from March 1947, as governor. Clay was known as the 'proconsul for Germany' and a 'benevolent despot'.[8]

Clay's initial attitude was clear. He told his staff they were in Germany to punish it and 'hold it down the way it should be'. But although the most consistent theme of JCS 1067 had been punishment, successive governors were given latitude to interpret it, and Clay soon softened his approach, impressed by the way in which the ordinary German people were seeking to tackle the devastation the war had left behind. Clay had a clear sense of

America's mission there. He actively intervened in all the important political matters. It was he, for example, who obliged Erhard to adopt a harsh rate of exchange for the DM, understanding that he, Clay, could dare to do what a German politician could not. Clay also insisted that the constitution be based on human rights and federal democracy. He once told his interpreter that he was proud of the beneficial impact he believed he had; he regretted only his failure to totally abolish class, the power of banks and of bureaucrats.[9]

As we have seen, Clay's first formal address to the minister-presidents of the US Länder was not only *not* unfriendly; it was intended to be fair, clear and, above all, to make it plain that the US would support every move to make liberal democracy function successfully in Germany. It is significant that for the US the Länder governments were the key institutions. They were established at the beginning of October 1945 and by 17 October their German chiefs, the minister-presidents, had their first meeting in Stuttgart with Clay.[10]

In their attitude towards the minister-presidents, important initial signs of Anglo-American differences on Germany can be seen. Whereas the Americans immediately focused on the Länder as the vital units (in order to encourage federalism) and requested their minister-presidents to come together to meet as a Länderrat, or Land council, the British chose to concentrate their efforts on centralising policy-making, and in identifying 'leading zonal personalities': men like Adenauer in Cologne and Fuchs in Düsseldorf. They wanted to run their zone from the top down – and the top meant British control, not the minister-presidents, even if a federal system rather than a unitary state proved to be the eventual goal of both the UK and the US. In this way, the British were content to let their Länder chiefs make their own moves to meet; they were then able to become a Zonenbeirat, or Zonal advisory council, but a body with less power and prestige than the American analogue.[11]

An early start was made in establishing political parties. Pressure to form them began to build up in all the zones soon after Germany's capitulation. There were several reasons for this. First, German democrats chose to perceive the Third Reich as a hiatus in German political life. They were keen to prove this by becoming active at once. Second, parties represented organised opinions and interests. However downtrodden and submissive the German people had become, there were some Germans with opinions. All of them had interests. Even where there was so very little to be consumed (perhaps precisely because there was very little) competition for what there was could be best articulated through parties. Above all, the Americans believed in democratic politics. It had been American intelligence officers who had first identified Adenauer: the beginning of a strong and fruitful relationship.[12] The Americans permitted licensed parties to start operating in August 1945.

At local level (as shown, for example, in Bavaria) the US intervened with a firm hand, first to punish and then to create democratic conditions. US polls of prisoners of war in Bavaria had shown that about 35 per cent of them were still active Nazis, 40 per cent passive Nazis, 10 per cent active resisters and 15 per cent passive resisters. The high figure of active and passive Nazis caused understandable alarm. Security demanded that Nazism be extirpated from German political life. JCS 1067 laid down that anyone who was more than a nominal Nazi would have to be dismissed.

In practice, it proved very difficult to de-Nazify the US zone and govern it at the same time. The waters were muddied somewhat by General Patton's famous observation that 'the Nazi thing was just like a Democratic and Republican election fight', and against this background the man appointed minister-president, Fritz Schäffer, a former prisoner in Dachau, had proposed that ex-Nazis should be allowed to serve in the bureaucracy for a three-year probationary period. However undesirable, there was little alternative to this policy if the administration was to be started up again.

The Americans were strongly opposed to the policy, favoured by the British government, of state ownership of key industries. They believed that far from endangering democracy, capitalism nurtured it and governments should not interfere. In 1945, learning about Erhard's views on the free market, they appointed him to the Bavarian government. His concept of free market activity combined with social responsibility contained, in their view, the only sensible basis for the economic future. When the people of Hesse, in the US zone, voted in June 1946 for a constituent assembly that decided to nationalise 169 coal and steel companies as well as the transport system, General Clay refused to accept the decision, and ordered what in effect was a plebiscite on 1 December on this issue. When this vote showed a 70 per cent majority for nationalisation (most of the Hesse Christian Democrats were in favour of the policy) Clay agreed to keep the clause in the constitution, but denied permission for it to be carried out.[13]

British policy

The British, as was perhaps to be expected from an imperial and colonial power, were determined to take occupation very seriously. The British dealt with the horrendous tasks that confronted them with efficiency, even if individual British leaders often found it hard to disguise their dislike of the

Germans. No less a figure than the British Foreign Minister, Ernest Bevin, was known to 'hate' Germans. Ivone Kirkpatrick wrote that

> one thing which left its mark upon him was the bellicose attitude of the German Social Democrats in 1914 for which he never forgave them. He felt betrayed and it made him more anti-German than anything else the Germans ever did. His post-war experience confirmed his gloomy view of German Social Democracy and he found Dr Adenauer much less difficult than Dr Schumacher . . . . [14]

But it was clear to any British official with any sense at all that hatred could not guide policy (and Bevin's personal views did not). The British zone was to be run as if it were a colony, or as Noel Annan put it in his personal memoir of the British occupation, as if the Germans were 'a specially intelligent tribe of Bedouins'.[15] Yet this does not mean quite what it seems. The colonial principle was to maintain overall control but devolve actual decision-making, and to encourage the emergence of domestic leaders whose aims ran parallel to those of Britain. Apart from the central themes of occupation laid down at Potsdam, the British, more than the other Allies, were content to let Germans shape their own destinies.

The British element of the Control Commission for Germany was at first headed by Field Marshal Montgomery. His deputy, General Sir Brian Robertson, succeeded him in 1947. In October 1945 a Minister for Germany, John Hynd, was appointed and almost 55,000 people were employed by the Control Commission for Germany. His headquarters (known as the 'hindquarters') was, however, in London; and he, not unwisely, chose a Jewish colleague, Austin Albu, to represent him in the Zone. As Annan put it, 'the Germans would recognise that a Jew had been sent to help in the resurrection of their country'.[16]

Cost, rising by early 1946 to £80 million a year, was a major British concern, not least because the Labour government of 1945 had embarked upon an over-ambitious programme of nationalisation. Another worry was the growing perception that the Soviet Union did not want to cooperate with the West, but was intent on extending the power of communism. Sir William Strang, political adviser to Montgomery, defined British tasks in what became the four British Länder as being first and foremost concerned with food, coal, displaced persons and public safety. The politics, he believed, could wait. He agreed with the plan to 'rebuild the life of the people on humane and decent lines'.

The situation facing the British in Germany was, of course, as chaotic as that which faced its allies. The supply of food was indeed a horrendous problem. Only America could prevent starvation. Its productive power also meant that it increasingly found itself required to dictate general economic policy. Here, too, there was a real difference between British and American thinking; here, too, the American view prevailed (to the ultimate advantage of the Germans). Thus Britain's Labour government decided in November 1946 to nationalise the Ruhr industries. The Americans and French disliked this policy and believed the British were taking decisions on a Land level that would influence Germany as a whole. Increasingly the Americans were prepared to insist the British heed their views. The effect was a go-slow on nationalisation. Despite the fact that the North Rhine-Westphalian Land Parliament voted in August 1946 in favour of the state ownership of the coal industry, the British now refused to accept the bill.

British policy was closer to American on political parties, which were permitted to establish themselves under licence in the UK zone from August 1945. On the whole, of all the occupying powers, the British seem to have given least thought to this particular matter. They considered Berlin to be the real centre of German political life and initially had relatively little understanding of or sympathy for those political groups whose roots lay not in national but in provincial political life. Although they recognised the existence of German social democracy, Britain's Labour leaders were not sympathetic to it. Whilst there is some evidence that ordinary occupation officials preferred the Social Democrats (SPD) to the Christian Democrats (CDU) because they were more radical and untainted by Nazism, there was no natural affinity towards German Socialists.

The British took a special interest in trade union affairs, however. They saw that General Zhukov in his Order No. 2 had established a 'Free German Trade Union' but noted quickly that this was to be communist. Even before 1945, British ministers, in particular Ernest Bevin, then Minister of Labour, had given thought to how to manage German trade union affairs. In Bevin's eyes, the strong support (as he saw it) that the British trade union movement was able to give the Labour Party was an important reason why the Labour Party was not the SPD.

Bevin planned for a genuinely free German trade union system in order to help teach the Germans how to be democrats. The British aim was not, as has sometimes been supposed, to form a single trade union for all workers, which they saw as a communist concept. In November 1945 a high-level delegation from the Trades Union Congress visited German trade unionists and despite much acrimony (the Germans were accused of having caved in to Nazism) told the Germans to come to their own conclusion about the best structure to adopt. The British were, however, adamant that there should be only one umbrella organisation for the German trade unions. They strongly supported the ideas of Hans Böckler that there should be one German trade union federation (DGB) and that it should consist of 13 autonomous industrial unions; and this was the origin of the trade union structure that has served Germans so well for half a century.

The clearest demonstration of Britain's centralising policy was the decision to form a new German political entity by creating a Rhine-Ruhr 'super' state, the Land of North Rhine-Westphalia. They believed that this conglomerate, with its proposed state-run industries, would be adopted as a model by other Länder. By July 1946 the British were ready to discuss the proposal with influential Germans. The CDU were not against it, since they saw in it a source of future strength for the decentralising element of federalism. The SPD, on the other hand, disliked the idea for the same reason. In August the British formally dissolved the Prussian western provinces and instituted the new Länder of Schleswig-Holstein, Lower Saxony and North Rhine-Westphalia. North Rhine-Westphalia proved (without state ownership of its industries) to be a highly prosperous unit which went on to provide much of the Federal Republic's economic prowess. The first Land elections in the British zone were held in April 1947.

British attempts to reform the civil service in their zone were subject to exactly the same constraints experienced by the Americans and French. The fact is that the professional German civil service managed, in the western part of Germany, to emerge from the Third Reich unscathed despite the many calls made for its complete reform. One recent German author, Curt Garner, has suggested that the German bureaucracy was a conservative elite, with no love of democracy; yet the western Allies failed to use the opportunities to remodel it so that by 1951 there were more civil servants who had possessed Nazi Party membership in the Foreign Office, for example, than there had been in 1940.[17] He accepts that the Americans, in particular, did make some changes in respect of gender equality (female civil servants could previously be dismissed on marriage) but he paints a dismal picture of a civil service that was, to put it mildly, insensitive about its corporate behaviour during the Third Reich.

There were certainly some civil servants, Adenauer's chief aide Globke being one of them, who ought to have distanced themselves from public life (though Globke was never a Nazi). It is also the case that West Germans tended to equate party membership for the senior political civil servants as proof that the service itself was 'democratic'. Yet the fact remains that the German civil service behaved quite properly and did not need greater politicisation to achieve what its political masters required it to do. Above all, de-Nazification meant that even if former Nazis could re-join the service, it was simply impossible for them to act as anything other than good democrats.

The need for de-Nazification was also a major problem for those responsible for education. Sixteen thousand teachers were banned in the British zone alone. Only one-third of the schools were left standing. But despite the shortage of teachers and accommodation, the big majority of children were back in school by the autumn of 1945 and the universities were beginning to open again. The British, determined to restart the education of the Germans by the Germans, had appointed anti-Nazi regional education authorities; and by the end of 1946 they passed responsibility for educational legislation to the Land assemblies. The British cultural policy was then confined to emphasising the merits of liberal democracy as a political value and addressing the problem of the Germans' isolation from decent cultural activities during the Third Reich.

A big effort was put into this longer-term cultural policy in the early postwar years. Distinguished speakers such as Sir William Beveridge and T.S. Eliot and many cultural manifestations were brought to Germany. A particularly successful aspect of the information policy was the establishment of newspapers. The British-licensed paper in Berlin was preferred by 40 per cent of the population, compared with 23 per cent for the American and 7 per cent for the Soviet one. *Die Welt, Die Zeit* and *Der Spiegel*, licensed in Hamburg during the British occupation, are still leading lights among the German press. But the policy of leaving matters as far as possible to the Germans, of being facilitators not dictators, while being in many ways enlightened, also had its downside. It went along with a certain aloofness and with a tendency to emphasise the Britishness and distinctiveness of British culture rather than to portray its contribution to European culture. American cultural policy as such may have been weaker, but the Germans found American culture much more accessible. The French, once they had decided to get on terms with the Germans, put an immense effort into their policy. Thus the Franco-German Treaty of 1963 emphasised cultural exchanges. Nearly 2 million French and Germans took part in youth exchanges in the next five years; and over 2.5 million have done so since then. Cultural policy on that scale cannot but underpin good political relations.

If the British were never able to make of their own input into German affairs the success that the Americans, and later the French, were able to score, this was not because they failed to make an impact in the early years, nor simply because they had far fewer resources than the Americans, but also because, sadly, they failed to build imaginatively upon it by accepting the possibilities for Britain that a real partnership in Europe might provide.

The Basic Law and the Bundesrepublik

By 1948 the Americans and the British felt they could openly develop western Germany into a state that could be part of the western community.[18] This policy was predicated on the growing conviction that Stalin's chief aims included the extension of Soviet power and influence as far west as possible. The communist-led coup in Prague in February 1948 confirmed this view and the first stirrings of communist aggression were observed in Korea in that year, too. The issue of German unity was subsumed in this wider struggle. In March 1948 the Brussels Treaty was signed in London, committing Britain, France and the Benelux countries to defence cooperation. At a further London conference of the same group of states it was announced on 1 June 1948 that it was now 'necessary to give the German people the opportunity to achieve on the basis of a free and democratic form of government, the eventual re-establishment of German unity at present disrupted'. To achieve this end, the military governors were ordered to hold meetings with the minister-presidents of the western zone to convene a constituent assembly with the task of preparing the West German constitution.

Clay had already in November 1947 produced a memorandum on a democratic and federal constitution for a single Germany, based on the constitutions used in the American zone, which was influential in the drafting of the constitutional Basic Law of the Federal Republic. By the spring of 1948 the Americans, British and French agreed that a constitutional assembly be set up to provide a draft within a year.[19] While the drafting was to be done by the Germans under the leadership of the minister-presidents, the Americans were particularly insistent that the constitution must embody an immutable commitment to human rights and democracy as well as a federal structure.

The federal division of powers between two levels of democratic government had been invented by the American Founding Fathers in order to prevent over-mighty central government, so support for it was natural for the Americans. Their preference for a decentralised federal system was shared by the CDU and by Adenauer in particular, with his 'disagreeable memories of Prussian rule over the Rhineland'.[20] The French, who had advocated a dismemberment of Germany, favoured a very loose confederation. British officials 'hardly understood the notion of federalism, despite the fact that the Colonial Office often imposed that form of government upon colonies that were gaining their independence'.[21] The British, with support from the SPD, favoured less decentralisation than the Americans and the CDU. Thus the question of federalism or centralisation was the most controversial when the draft came before the Allied governors in February 1949 for their approval. But the Americans, the CDU and most of the minister-presidents of the Länder, who had more influence in the matter than the emerging national leaders, obtained the federal constitution they desired.

While the Americans had insisted that the draft should not be subject to a plebiscite before entering into force, the Allies were concerned that the constitution should be seen to emanate from the German people; and it was indeed the work of the German Constituent Assembly, subject to the approval of the Allied governors, which was accepted with only minor alterations.[22] The essential elements of a federal system as pioneered by the Americans were retained: a constitutional court, a two-chamber legislature to represent respectively the citizens and the states/Länder, a federal executive, a guarantee of rights and a division of powers entrenched in the constitution. But other features reflected German traditions, such as the representation of Land governments rather than specially elected representatives or 'senators' in the Bundesrat; the important role of the Land administrators in the execution of federal policy; and, as in Britain and most other European countries, a parliamentary not a presidential executive. Such features have commended themselves to other Europeans too, in designing the institutions of the European Community.

What did occupation achieve?

The general case that has been made against the western occupying powers is that they failed to radically change the nature of German political life. Both German and non-German observers note the existence of political continuity within Germany from the Weimar period to the Bonn Republic, exemplified by the personal careers of men like Adenauer and Schumacher. This is regarded as straightforward restoration of the Germany democracy of the Weimar years, with some important changes, but minimal anglo-saxon input. In addition, there has been criticism constructed on the failure to socialise German industry, reform the bureaucracy and education system, or establish a welfare state along British lines. In fact such criticism is wholly misplaced. There was no way in which the British or any of the other western Allies could coerce the Germans to support any one particular party. The Germans, it was thought, needed to be educated in order to behave democratically: that could not be done against their will, without refuting the very principle the western Allies sought to uphold. Any critique of any individual policy must be set against the successful establishment of liberal democracy and the processes of de-Nazification. These totally changed the basis for German political life. Even if too many undesirable individuals were left in important places, their capacity to do serious harm had all but vanished.

The fact is that occupation policy wrought the most tremendous and positive changes on German political life. It secured the fortunes of genuine democracy in Germany. It purged and criminalised Nazism. It renewed and consolidated federalism. It supported a German economy that was liberal, market oriented and open. It led to a Germany that became a pillar of the European Union and of the North Atlantic Treaty Organisation. West Germany and its values were products made by the western Allies, in particular the United States, to a far greater extent than either they or the West Germans would subsequently accept. The origins of the Federal Republic lay more in Washington, London and Paris than in Bonn.

To those who argue that what the West did was therefore no different from what the Soviet Union did in its zone of Germany, it must be pointed out that the Soviet Union was a totalitarian state, thus far more radical in its approach to German affairs, and that this had ultimately no lasting impact. The reason is perhaps that democracy can no more be relativised than dictatorship, whether of a party or a person, or both. Nor should we forget that the westernisation of West Germany was legitimated in free elections in every single local and federal election since 1946.

The Federal Republic did not just happen: it was made in accord with anglo-saxon guidelines – and stipulations. French plans for dismemberment were eschewed just as decisively as Soviet ones to make a communist German nation. Things were done to German political life which the Germans could not, and would not, have done for themselves, though the other side of the coin was equally essential: enough Germans were able and willing to play their part. This allowed a certain sort of Germany in the west to be established which has proved a model democracy.

The way in which democracy was installed under supervision, and subsequently gained the support of ordinary Germans, indicates a number of political truths. Two of them stand out: first, that nations can learn to change their ways; second, that other nations can help them do so, even if this may occur, to the extent that it did in postwar Germany, only in exceptional circumstances. Fifty years ago Germany was subject to an education in how to be western and a good European. Britain was one of its teachers. Today, perhaps, Britain should be the pupil and Germany may need to provide some of the teaching.

8 The European Parliament and the Idea of European Representative Government
Richard Corbett MEP

Two main strands of thought lay behind the idea that an elected assembly or Parliament should be among the institutions of what is now the European Union. One arose directly from the principles of representative government, seeking to apply them to the new European entity being created. It was concerned with the *nature* of this entity: given the scope of its responsibilities and decision-taking powers, it was felt necessary to ensure that the Community should not be the exclusive preserve of government ministers and officials, but that there should be scope for the plurality of views and interests offered by a Parliament. For federalists, the elected Parliament would, together with the Council as a house of the states, comprise the federal legislature. In line with the principles of representative government, the laws would be enacted by the legislature, to which a federal executive would be accountable, while the rule of law would be upheld by a federal judiciary. The second strand of thought was connected with the *process* of European integration, linked to the belief that an assembly could play a decisive role in furthering that process.

For many federalists, both these strands were important. They drew much of their inspiration from what Altiero Spinelli, one of the co-founders of the European federalist movement, called 'the great American political experience'.[1] He made no secret of the fact that his ideas were derived from the works of British federalists such as William Beveridge, Lord Lothian, Lionel Robbins and Barbara Wootton, who had been active in the Federal Union movement in the late 1930s. 'Their analysis of the political and economic perversion to which nationalism leads', he was to write, 'and their reasoned presentation of the federal alternative, have remained to this day impressed on my memory like a revelation. Since I was looking for mental clarity and precision, I was not attracted by the foggy and contorted ideological federalism of a Proudhon or a Mazzini, but by the clean, precise thinking of these English federalists . . . .'[2] The institutions which the British federalists recommended were based on those devised by the American Founding Fathers at the Philadelphia Convention, save that, following British and other European traditions, they leant towards a parliamentary rather than a presidential executive. Spinelli and most of the others who shaped the thinking of the postwar European federalists took a similar view of the institutions that would be required.

Proposals for a European constitution

Many of the postwar federalists, most notably Spinelli, were inspired by the example of the Philadelphia Convention to envisage a European constituent assembly that would draw up a federal constitution. The European Parliamentary Union, composed of parliamentarians from many European countries and led by its founder, Richard Coudenhove-Kalergi, who had returned from exile in America in 1946 and was also highly influenced by the American tradition, likewise advocated a constituent assembly.[3] Support for the idea was strong among the peoples of continental countries who had suffered defeat and occupation. But those, such as the British, whose confidence in the nation-state had not been so severely shaken, were generally sceptical, even if it proved possible in April 1948 to secure the signatures of nearly 200 MPs, with both Conservatives and Labour strongly represented, to a motion calling for a long-term policy to create a European federation, to be designed by a constituent assembly which the West European governments should convene as soon as possible.[4]

The continental governments too, as they recovered their authority and confidence, became increasingly resistant to such a radical transformation. But those of France, West Germany, Italy and the Benelux countries were willing to take important steps in a federal direction. Jean Monnet was the pioneer among those federalists who sought the support of governments and interests that were ready to take such steps, without necessarily committing themselves to the end-product of a federation. He initiated the launching in May 1950 of the Schuman Plan that led to the creation of the European Coal and Steel Community (ECSC), which in turn provided the foundation on which to build the European Union of today, including its main representative bodies: the Council representing the states and the European Parliament representing the citizens. As Spinelli observed at the time, the institutions that Monnet successfully proposed for the ECSC foreshadowed the government, Parliament and court of a 'true and proper federal state'.[5]

The Assembly of the Council of Europe

The Assembly of the ECSC, which was to develop into today's European Parliament, was not, however, the first European parliamentary assembly to be established. That honour belongs to the Council of Europe, set up following The Hague Congress of European Organisations which, in May

1948, brought together representatives of all the various movements supporting European unity. Some 700 personalities participated, including a dozen former or future prime ministers or presidents. Despite the caution of the British government towards this event, some 50 Westminster MPs took part (22 Labour and 23 Conservative). Besides Winston Churchill, who was the star speaker of the Congress, Anthony Eden, Harold Macmillan, Ronald Mackay and Duncan Sandys played an important part in the proceedings, as did former French prime ministers Paul Ramadier and Paul Reynaud, future German chancellor Konrad Adenauer, former Belgian prime minister Paul van Zeeland and Princess Juliana of the Netherlands. Participants came from across Europe, though most were from the Benelux countries, Britain and France.

The Congress revealed the divergence between the inter-governmentalist view of European organisation, whose most important exponents were in the British delegation, and the federalist view which was prevalent among the continentals, though also shared by a number of the British, led by Ronald Mackay, a Labour MP who had in April promoted the federalist resolution in the House of Commons and was to be a leading exponent of the federalist view in the Council of Europe's Assembly. In the final resolution, the Congress agreed unanimously that a 'European Assembly chosen by the Parliaments of the participating nations' be convened;[6] and an Assembly was duly established as an institution of the Council of Europe in 1949. The character of the Assembly was again the subject of conflict between inter-governmentalists, led by the British government, who wanted it to have minimal powers, with its members appointed by their governments and sitting in national delegations that would vote as national blocs, against the more federalist view of some of Britain's closest continental neighbours who wanted an autonomous assembly with significant powers, elected by the member-states' Parliaments. While the British managed to ensure that the Council of Europe's Assembly would be merely consultative, with the powers concentrated in the Council of Ministers, it was the first parliamentary assembly to be established in any significant international organisation. Its creation formed a precedent: all subsequent European organisations would have one too. It also created precedents in winning some of its early battles: members to vote as individuals and not in national blocs, the right to fix its own agenda, and a degree of operational autonomy. Such features were subsequently of crucial importance to the European Parliament. The Assembly also provided a forum which, especially for the first two years of its existence, was of great significance in debating further moves towards European unity, paving the way for the Schuman Plan. The establishment of parliamentary assemblies in the Council of Europe and subsequently the

Community meant that 'Parliamentarians for the first time participated in (the external representation) of the State. Parliamentary action began to replace diplomatic action. This gradually changed relations in Europe from a character of foreign policy to a character of home policy, from international law to constitutional law.'[7] Europe was not to be an exclusive domain for ministers, diplomats and bureaucrats. Elected parliamentarians were also to play their part.

A Parliament for the European Community

It was André Philip, a French socialist deputy who had been prominent in the federalist cause in the Council of Europe's Assembly, who put to Monnet the idea that the ECSC too should have its parliamentary assembly.[8] In his inaugural speech as president of the Community's High Authority, Monnet, pointing out that this executive was responsible to the Assembly, which had the right to withdraw confidence and thus to dismiss it, affirmed that it was 'the first European Assembly endowed with sovereign powers'; and, together with the Court of Justice and the High Authority, comprised 'supranational and, let us say the word, federal institutions'.[9] Monnet, too, had lived for many years in America and was, like Spinelli, strongly influenced by the American political experience. In the same debate, Chancellor Adenauer, speaking as president of the Council, said that this 'first sovereign parliament established on a supranational basis' was in a relationship with Council 'comparable, in certain respects, to the relations between two chambers in the constitutional life of a state'.[10]

The ECSC Treaty, like the Rome Treaty establishing the European Economic Community (EEC), provided for the future direct elections of the Assembly. But although the Rome Treaty gave the EEC substantial legislative power, the governments were initially reluctant to give any of this power to the Assembly, preferring to keep it in their own hands, at their meetings in the Council of Ministers; and they likewise kept a tight rein on executive powers, which were not fully bestowed upon the Commission, as the EEC's executive was named. While the European Parliament, as it came to be called, had the draconian power to dismiss the Commission as a whole, when it came to legislation and the budget it was given only a consultative status.

The result was that the European Community system contained a Parliament which, unlike most national Parliaments, did not regard itself as part of a finished institutional system, but as part of one requiring evolution or even transformation into something different, seeking to turn the Community from a largely intergovernmental system to one based more on parliamentary principles. While not all of its members have subscribed to the end-product of a federation, the Parliament as a whole has played an important part in promoting the process of integration in that direction.

Parliament's vocation to promote constitutional change was recognised and encouraged in its first session in 1952 when Chancellor Adenauer, speaking on behalf of the Council of Ministers, invited it to draft a Treaty for a European Political Community. Parliament, given a few extra members and designated as the 'ad hoc Assembly' for this purpose, proceeded to do so. Although its project fell with the demise of the European Defence Community in 1954, many of its proposals served in the negotiation of the EEC Treaty two years later.

Parliament continued to press both to improve and develop Community policies and to strengthen its position within the institutional framework of the Community, whether through undertakings from Council and from the Commission, through interpretation of the Treaties, through inter-institutional agreements supplementing the Treaties or even through treaty amendments. Parliament also pressed for many years for the implementation of the treaty provision regarding its own direct election by universal suffrage. The final achievement of this objective in 1979, on the basis of a proposal drawn up in Parliament by Dutch Labour MEP Schelto Patijn, was itself a major constitutional change in the Community, but was one which had been hotly debated before its implementation.

Direct elections were supported by those who saw an elected Parliament fulfilling the functions of democratic scrutiny directly at European level as a natural step in the Community's institutional framework, or as part of the process of integration. This was strongly argued by the European federalist movement, but not by all those who would describe themselves as federalists. Hendrik Brugmans, for instance, argued that the first need was to create a strong European executive, and then to establish a Parliament to control it.[11] Sicco Mansholt, former President of the Commission, asked whether it was really desirable to organise elections to a Parliament without powers.[12] Indeed, many felt that direct elections should come only after the Parliament was given genuine powers. For others, direct elections would be crucial in securing those powers. For Georges Vedel, 'the birth act of Europe will be signed only the day when European elections by direct universal suffrage take place, the rest can follow: the extension of the powers of the Parliament and the constitution of an executive . . . But we must start with elections.'[13]

It is therefore not surprising that direct elections initially had an ambiguous effect. Although they conferred upon the Parliament a greater 'legitimacy' in that its Members could justly claim to be the only directly elected Community institution, representing the peoples of the Community at

European level, on the other hand they did provoke, especially in some member-states, a somewhat negative public reaction. The public had, after all, been called upon to choose its representatives in an assembly which did not have a decisive say in Community decisions. Electors who, in the national context, were used to parliamentary elections that are in practice about the performance of governments and whether to change them, suddenly found themselves having to vote for a Parliament that could not elect or change a government. This new political animal was all too easily misunderstood by the public, and was a ready target for those opposed to the European Community who were not keen on seeing a stronger European Parliament.

Nevertheless, direct elections were a step forward for the Parliament. In transforming it into a full-time body they created a new class of politicians in Europe. Within almost every political party there was now a small, but not insignificant, number of politicians whose career depended on making something of the European dimension. They acted as essential go-betweens in explaining the Community and its potential to national parties and in bringing national parties further into European discussions. Most MEPs also established networks of contacts in their constituencies and in the civil society and began to develop the sort of representative role that members of national Parliaments fulfil in the more established (and, still, more significant) national context.[14]

The European Parliament has also constantly pressed for institutional changes, generally promoting three distinct but related objectives. First, Parliament has sought to clarify and where necessary strengthen the competences and responsibilities of the European Community itself. Parliament has consistently argued that powers should be attributed to the Community on the basis of the principle of subsidiarity: that is to say that it should exercise those responsibilities, and only those responsibilities, that can be carried out more effectively by common policies at Community level than by the member-states acting separately. It is an indication of how far Parliament has influenced the political debate that this rather ungainly expression, 'principle of subsidiarity', has become part of the political vocabulary, as it was a term virtually unknown in the English language until Parliament started to use it in the early 1980s.

Second, Parliament has argued that those responsibilities which are exercised at Community level should be carried out more effectively than at present. Here Parliament has been particularly critical of the practice of unanimity in the Council of Ministers, arguing that, where it has been agreed to conduct a policy jointly, it makes no sense to give a blocking power to each of the component states of the Community. The unanimity rule has been described as dictatorship of the minority. Parliament has also pleaded for a stronger role to be given to the Commission in carrying out policies once they have been agreed. Both developments would move away from inter-governmentalism to a more majoritarian system.

Third, and most significantly from the perspective of this chapter, Parliament has pleaded for better democratic control and accountability at Community level. It argued that those responsibilities which national Parliaments, in ratifying the treaties, have transferred to the Community should not be exercised by the Council (i.e. national ministers) alone: that the loss of parliamentary powers at the national level to the governments' representatives in the Council should be compensated by an increase in parliamentary power at European level. Parliament has sought to have a power of co-decision with Council on Community legislation so that ministers' legislative decisions in the Council would enter into force only with the explicit approval of a public vote in an elected assembly. Co-decision would not allow Parliament to impose legislation on the member-states which their representatives in Council did not want. It would, however, require Council to ensure that it had the agreement of the representatives which the electorate has chosen directly at that level, for any legislation which it desires.

Such a change, combined with greater parliamentary power over the appointment of the Commission (which it already had the power to dismiss), and the reinforcement of the Commission mentioned above, would move the Community towards having a bicameral legislative and budgetary authority (Council, representing the states, and Parliament, directly representing the electorate) and an executive (the Commission) accountable to it: indeed, to apply the principles of representative government.

Achievements of the nominated Parliament

Already the unelected Parliament, composed of seconded national parliamentarians, which existed until 1979 pressed to achieve those objectives. Three main steps were achieved before or, in the last case, around the time of direct elections in that year.

First, the budget treaties of 1970 and 1975 created what amounts to a bicameral 'budgetary authority', composed of Council and Parliament, which jointly thrashes out agreement on the annual Community budget within a fixed revenue limit. Although the budget procedures are complicated, they are significant. They allow Parliament to amend, and over the years reshape, the budget. Although the budget is still relatively small (less than 4 per cent of total public expenditure in the Union), Parliament has managed, by using its powers, to allocate expenditure in areas other than agriculture and thereby to develop Community policies in new areas.

This development was linked to one of the 'constitutional' developments of the Union; namely, the introduction of the Community's 'own resources' replacing national budgetary contributions 'with tax revenue allocated once and for all to the Community and accruing to it automatically without the need for any subsequent decision by national authorities'.[15]

The treaties' provision for such 'own resources' to be raised in order to cover the Community's expenditure was seen by federalists as an essential instrument of governance, preventing a member-state from holding the Community to ransom by withholding its national contribution. The common external tariff and the agricultural import levies, which were initially the main sources of revenue, could moreover hardly accrue to the state collecting them, when they resulted from common policies and could, indeed, be levied on goods in transit. By 1966 the common agricultural policy began to generate substantial expenditure. But the treaties required the system of own resources, and the ceiling for budgetary revenue, to be adopted by all the member-states 'in accordance with their respective constitutional requirements' (Article 201 EEC); and the Dutch Parliament made it clear that it would not approve any budgetary system that failed to provide for parliamentary approval of the resulting public expenditure.

The Dutch insistence on control of the executive's expenditure by a body representing the citizens had deep roots in the history of the Netherlands, as Chapter 3 of this volume has shown. Since common expenditure could not be controlled by the several Parliaments of the member-states, it would have to be controlled by the European Parliament.[16] This idea was anathema to President de Gaulle, who created the 'empty chair' crisis in the Council when it was proposed by the Commission and supported by the other five member-states in 1966, and who refused to accept it so long as he remained president of France, insisting on the retention of national contributions. But there was no way in which the Dutch Parliament and government could be shifted from their principled stand; and the Dutch were supported by the Belgian, German and Italian Parliaments and governments. Most of the budgetary expenditure was moreover for the common agricultural policy, and thus of great interest to France. By 1970, after De Gaulle's demise, the six member-states were able to agree on an amending treaty that gave some power over the expenditure of own resources to the European Parliament; and, to secure ratification by the member-states that wanted a stronger role for the Parliament than that treaty offered, a further amending treaty was promised, which was finally signed in 1975 and gave the Parliament powers more or less equal to those of the Council over most items of expenditure save agriculture, where the Parliament's role remained reduced. The 'power of the purse' has often been a crucial element in developing parliamentary government, and these two treaties were a breakthrough in the development of the European Parliament.

The second step coincided with the budgetary treaty of 1975, when a conciliation procedure was introduced, applying to legislation with budgetary consequences where there was a need to avoid potential conflict between Council's legislative powers and Parliament's budgetary powers. The procedure was established by a Joint Declaration, a sort of constitutional convention, between the institutions. It laid down that should Council wish to diverge from the opinion of the European Parliament with respect to a legislative proposal, the matter should first be referred to a conciliation committee composed of the members of Council and an equal number of MEPs.

The procedure resembles that of the Conciliation Committee (Vermittlungsausschuss) in the Federal Republic of Germany, where one Minister for each Land from the Bundesrat meets with an equivalent-sized delegation from the Bundestag to seek compromises where the positions of the two chambers diverge. The difference was that in the Community, at the end of the negotiations, whatever the result, it was up to one side, namely the Council, to adopt the act in question. The procedure was therefore more like an appeal for clemency in which MEPs could ask the national ministers in Council to think again. None the less, it did strengthen the Parliament's legislative role and provided a precedent for future conciliation procedures which have become more effective as the Parliament's powers have increased.

The third step resulted from the ruling of the Court of Justice with respect to the 'isoglucose' cases (138/79 and 139/79), when the Court struck down a piece of Community legislation because Council had adopted it before Parliament gave its opinion. The Court ruled that the provisions in the treaty requiring consultation of Parliament are

> the means which allows Parliament to play an actual part in the legislative process of the Community. Such a power represents an essential factor in the institutional balance intended by the Treaty. Although limited, it reflects at Community level the fundamental principle that the peoples should take part in the exercise of power through the intermediary of a representative assembly. Due consultation of the Parliament in the cases provided for by the Treaty therefore constitutes an essential formality, disregard of which means that the measure concerned is void.

This ruling gave Parliament a de facto delaying power. The Parliament immediately tried to build on that by amending its internal Rules of Procedure. An amended set of rules was drawn up by Hans Löcker, a German Christian Democrat MEP. It provided for Parliament, when dealing with the Commission's proposals, first to vote on the amendments it wishes to make to them, and then, before voting on the resolution as a whole which formally constitutes its opinion, seek an undertaking from the Commission that its amendments will be incorporated into the proposal. If this undertaking is not forthcoming, Parliament can delay its final vote, preventing a decision in Council. In such cases, the matter is referred back to the relevant parliamentary committee while compromises are sought.

Clearly, Parliament's bargaining position is stronger when there is pressure for a rapid decision. In such circumstances, even the consultation procedures can give Parliament some muscle in the legislative process. But Parliament's role still fell far short of what federalists, as well as many others, held to be necessary.

The draft treaty on European Union and the Single European Act

The elected Parliament took up its legacy with new vigour. The most important initiative of the first elected Parliament was its proposal in 1984 for a new treaty on European Union. In this initiative, Parliament was encouraged by Altiero Spinelli, by then an MEP. Spinelli had, ever since the 1950s, nurtured the idea of a constituent assembly elected by European citizens to draw up a federal constitution. Now that the directly elected Parliament had provided the citizens' representatives, he wanted them to produce a constitutional document that would go as far as possible in that direction. But he first had to persuade a somewhat cautious Parliament to take such a radical initiative. A first circular letter to MEPs brought a response from only eight others: Richard Balfe, Paola Gaiotti, Stanley Johnson, Brian Key, Silvio Leonardi, Hans Löcker, Bruno Vissentini and Karl von Wogau: all British, German or Italian. They founded the 'Crocodile Club', named after the restaurant in which they first met. Within a few months, it had further support, not least from Willy Brandt, Rudy Arndt, Martin Bangemann, Bruno Friedrich, Horst Seefeld, Heidi Wieczorek-Zeul, Leo Tindemans, Hans Nord and Susanna Agnelli. The Crocodile Club persuaded Parliament to set up a special committee on Institutional Affairs in 1982 for this purpose. Spinelli became its general rapporteur, leading a team of six co-rapporteurs covering different sectors and representing the main Political Groups (Karel De Gucht, Jacques Moreau, Gero Pfenning, Derek Prag, Hans-Joachim Seeler and Ortensio Zecchino).

The committee held public hearings and its drafts were circulated through party political networks. By September 1983, Parliament was able to approve a lengthy resolution specifying the contents that such a new treaty should have, including full co-decision of the Parliament with the Council on legislation and responsibility of the Commission to the Parliament, in line with the principles of representative government. The committee, with the assistance of a team of legal experts, then transformed this into a draft treaty which was adopted on 14 February 1984 by a vote of 237 to 31. This huge majority reflected the careful work of compromise and consensus-building that had taken place among the main Groups. Spinelli's approach had been based on thrashing out a political compromise among the main political forces in Europe on the grounds that this was more likely to lead to genuine progress than the traditional method of preparing treaties by working parties of officials from foreign ministries.

Adopting a draft treaty was one thing: gaining support for it was another. Parliament pursued four main channels in trying to build up support: directly to governments, both individually and collectively in the European Council of Heads of State or Government; through national political parties that had to take a position on the issue in their policy statements and manifestos for the 1984 European election, and which would have to bear in mind how their MEPs had voted; through national Parliaments, which were invited to support the initiative and to each of which the European Parliament sent delegations to explain and seek support; and through interest groups, non-governmental organisations and academia by supporting and responding to the considerable interest stimulated in these circles by the draft treaty.

Generally positive reactions were immediately forthcoming from heads of government of Belgium, Germany, Italy and the Netherlands. By far the most significant reaction, however, was that of President Mitterrand, speaking as president of the European Council to the European Parliament on May 24. In a major turning point in French attitudes towards European integration, his speech culminated in an expression of support for the draft treaty, stating: 'France, ladies and gentlemen, is available for such an enterprise. I, on its behalf, state its willingness to examine and defend your project, the inspiration behind which it approves. I therefore suggest that preparatory consultations leading up to a conference of the member-states concerned be started up.'[17] This speech placed the draft treaty firmly on the political agenda. It is not without significance that, a couple of weeks before, he had met with Spinelli and Piet Dankert, president of the European Parliament.

At the subsequent Fontainebleau European Council, it was agreed to set up an ad hoc committee of personal representatives of the heads of state or governments, modelled on the Spaak Committee which had paved the way to the negotiation of the EEC Treaty in the 1950s. The committee was instructed to put forward proposals on institutional matters to the European Council. Some heads of government nominated MEPs or former MEPs to represent them on the committee. These included Enrico Ferri, former chairman of Parliament's Committee on Institutional Affairs, and Fernand Herman, subsequently the rapporteur of some of the committee's key reports. The committee also had meetings with the president of Parliament (by then Pierre Pflimlin) and Spinelli. The work of the ad hoc committee finally led to the adoption of a report which agreed with Parliament on the need for a new treaty establishing European Union. It recommended that this treaty be based on the existing Communities, the Stuttgart Solemn Declaration, and be 'guided by the spirit and the method of the draft treaty voted by the European Parliament'.[18] As regards the substance of this treaty, there were striking similarities between the proposals of the ad hoc committee and the European Parliament's draft treaty. However, three members of the ad hoc committee, the representatives from the UK, Denmark and Greece, stated publicly that they did not accept the main conclusions of the committee's report.

The report was considered at the meeting of the European Council in Milan in June 1985. By then, several national Parliaments had lent their support to the European Parliament's draft treaty. In Belgium and Italy, the Parliaments had adopted resolutions calling for it to be ratified as such. In Germany and the Netherlands, and in the French Parliament's responsible organs, more general support was forthcoming, urging their respective governments to open negotiations on the basis of the draft treaty. Even in member-states not noted for their enthusiasm, the proposals were taken seriously. Thus the House of Lords set up a special sub-committee to consider the issue, which held public hearings, including one with Spinelli, and concluded that some treaty changes were desirable.

The Milan European Council decided by a majority vote to convene an inter-governmental conference (IGC) to revise the existing treaties in accordance with the procedures set out in Article 236 of the EEC Treaty (requiring, ultimately, unanimous ratification by the member-states of any treaty changes). During the autumn of 1985, the member-states pursued negotiations based on the report of the ad hoc committee as well as the Commission's proposals for creating the single market, which eventually led to the Single European Act. The three reluctant states were, in the end, willing to negotiate compromises rather than be isolated.

During the negotiations, Parliament carefully monitored the work of the IGC. Its President and Spinelli were invited to two of the ministerial level meetings of the conference, but mainly informal contacts were used. The IGC had agreed to submit the results of its work to the European Parliament, and this was done in January 1986, before the signature of the text by the member-states. Indeed, Italy had indicated that it would not ratify the Act if the European Parliament rejected it. Parliament, although considering the results to be insufficient, nevertheless accepted them. The Single European Act was signed in February 1986 and, after ratification by all the member-states, came into force in July 1987.

The Single European Act increased the powers of the European Parliament in the legislative process by introducing two new procedures.

One was the 'cooperation procedure'. This applied initially to only ten treaty articles, but they covered most of the legislation necessary for the completion of the single market as well as individual research programmes and the rules for the structural funds. This procedure in effect added a second reading to the traditional consultation procedure, and by doing so enhanced Parliament's influence over legislation. Under the procedure, Council's decision, now known as a 'common position', was referred back to Parliament, which had three months to approve it, reject it (in which case it fell unless Council then overruled Parliament by unanimity within three months) or press for amendments (which, if supported by the Commission, could only be rejected unanimously in Council, whereas a qualified majority could approve). This procedure resulted in the adoption of some 300 acts in the first five years of its operation, in the course of which Council accepted some 2000 parliamentary amendments.

The Single Act also required Parliament's assent for the ratification of accession treaties and association agreements. Accession treaties are relatively infrequent events and the Parliament did not have an opportunity to use its power in this area until May 1994 when it approved the accession of Austria, Finland and Sweden. On the other hand, association agreements have arisen more frequently, not least because subsequent protocols (for example, financial protocols), which require renewing under the basic agreements, also fall under the assent procedure. Thus in the first year of operation of the Single Act, Parliament dealt with 26 such protocols.

Again, the European Parliament sought to maximise its new powers by rewriting its Rules of Procedure. This time, the rapporteur was Sir Christopher Prout, later leader of the British Conservatives in the Parliament. Sir Christopher drafted a set of rules that sought to interpret the new treaty provisions in such a way as to allow Parliament to amplify and fully exploit the opportunities offered. British MEPs were again prominent among those pressing for an enhanced parliamentary role at European level, despite the reticence of their own government.

From the Single European Act to the Treaty of Maastricht

Following the entry into force of the Single Act, the European Parliament began to campaign for a further process of reform. Between 1987 and the 1989 European elections, it adopted a series of reports aiming to show the insufficiencies of the Community's constitutional system as it resulted from the Single Act. These culminated in a report on Parliament's strategy for achieving European Union, in which Parliament argued for a new constitutional revision and recommended that the Parliament should itself prepare a proposal for this.[19]

Initially, the member-states were not interested in reopening negotiations on the treaty so soon after the Single Act. However, pressures were emerging in some fields as a direct consequence of the Single Act and the creation of a single European market. This was above all the case in the monetary field, where a majority of member-states came round to the view that a single market would require a single currency and that it was time to move forward on the Community's long-standing commitment to economic and monetary union. In June 1989, the European Council agreed to the principle of a new inter-governmental conference to consider proposals for this.

The European Parliament pressed for a wider agenda for the IGC. It adopted a resolution to that effect in November 1989 and its Institutional Committee began to prepare drafts of specific proposals for treaty amendments, with British Labour MEP David Martin, a vice-president of Parliament, as rapporteur. At the same time, Parliament defined its strategy to enlist support for this, proposing direct dialogue with Council in an inter-institutional conference and envisaging a conference of all the national Parliaments and the European Parliament, which became known as the 'assizes' and was held in Rome in November 1990.

Parliament's proposals were again based on the triptych of broader Community competence in accordance with the principle of subsidiarity, more effective decision-taking particularly through extending majority voting in Council, and greater democratic accountability notably by increasing the powers of the European Parliament. On this latter point, the Martin reports spelt out proposals for a co-decision procedure, designed to give Parliament powers equivalent to those of the Council with respect to legislation, and for involving Parliament in the appointment of the Commission.[20]

These proposals gradually gained wider support. First the Italian Parliament, then the Belgian government gave backing to them. In April 1990, Chancellor Kohl and President Mitterrand, spurred by the need to anchor a united Germany yet more firmly to the Community, wrote jointly to the other heads of government calling for a second IGC on political union. In June 1990, the European Council agreed to the principle of such an IGC to run parallel to that on economic and monetary union, but without defining in great detail what it should deal with. The following months were spent filling out its agenda, and Parliament's proposals in the Martin reports played an important part in the process. The assizes, held the month before the IGCs opened, were particularly successful from the European Parliament's point of view in that they led to the adoption, by 150 votes to 13, of a declaration that took up all of its main proposals for treaty revision. All the member-states' Parliaments participated in the week-long assizes, held in the Camera dei Deputati in Rome, where they provided two-thirds of the delegates, with one-third provided by the European Parliament.

During the IGCs, the European Parliament maintained its involvement through the inter-institutional conference that continued in parallel with them, with monthly meetings between the twelve ministers on the one hand and twelve MEPs on the other; and Parliament's president was able to address the meetings of the IGCs at ministerial level a number of times. Parliament's delegation toured the national capitals holding individual meetings with each head of government, pressing Parliament's case for reform.

The resulting Treaty of Maastricht, which established the European Union with the Community at its centre, flanked by two inter-governmental 'pillars' for common foreign and security policy and for cooperation in justice and home affairs, was again a compromise that included major steps in the direction advocated by the European Parliament. The institutional reforms included a modest extension of qualified majority voting in Council and the Court of Justice was given the power to impose fines on member-states failing to respect its judgments. The European Parliament's powers of scrutiny and control were increased in a number of ways:

- the treaty introduced the procedure of 'co-decision', based on the cooperation procedure, but with two important additional provisions: first, the inclusion of a formal conciliation committee for negotiating a compromise between the Council and the Parliament; and second, the option for the Parliament to reject proposals outright, thus causing the legislation to fall. This procedure applied to most legislation for which the Single European Act had stipulated the cooperation procedure, together with a number of new areas; and here the Council and Parliament were to comprise a legislature of two chambers on a fairly equal footing.

- the cooperation procedure was applied to most of the other areas where Council acts by a qualified majority
- the assent procedure was extended to a wider category of international agreements and a number of other areas
- Parliament gained a number of rights enshrined in the treaties in relation to appointments. It was formally invited to hold a vote on the nominations for the president of the Commission (legally consultative but politically hard to contest) and the president of the European Central Bank, and to give a vote of confidence in the Commission as a whole (whose normal term of office became linked to that of the Parliament). Thus the procedures for ensuring the Commission's responsibility to Parliament were substantially strengthened. The Parliament was also given the task of selecting an ombudsman whose five-year term of office, like that of the Commission, coincides with that of the Parliament
- various powers of scrutiny were enhanced, notably by a provision in the treaty for parliamentary committees of inquiry.

From Maastricht to Amsterdam

Following the Maastricht Treaty, Parliament continued to press for constitutional change. It secured no more than minor changes when the accession treaties of Austria, Finland and Sweden were negotiated. These changes included its proposals regarding the order of rotation of the Council presidency and the adaptation of the threshold for qualified majority voting; and its proposal on the number of MEPs for the new member-states was followed, apart from an extra seat for Austria. The Institutional Affairs Committee also prepared a draft constitution,[21] partly in response to a referendum held in Italy in 1989 in which 88 per cent of Italian voters favoured a mandate for the Parliament to produce one. Although this text was not specifically voted on by the plenary of Parliament, which merely took note of it, it did lay down a marker for future reforms and for the consolidation of the various treaties into a single constitutional text. Following the 1994 European elections, Parliament turned its attention to the intergovernmental conference scheduled by the Maastricht Treaty to be convened in 1996. The treaty specified that this IGC should examine, inter alia, the extension of the co-decision procedure to other areas, and whether fully to integrate the common foreign and security policy and cooperation in the fields of justice and home affairs into the Community legal system.

The European Council agreed in June 1994 to set up a 'Reflection Group' to prepare the IGC, composed of a representative of each foreign minister and two MEPs, enabling Parliament to participate directly in the preparations. Its two representatives were Elisabeth Guigou, former French European affairs minister (Socialist) and Elmar Brok (Christian Democrat). Its initial proposals were prepared by its Committee on Institutional Affairs with Jean-Louis Bourlanges and, again, David Martin as rapporteurs. They were adopted in May 1995 and, in line with Parliament's long-standing ideas on the European institutions, called for the generalisation of co-decision and qualified majority voting, stronger participation of the Parliament in the choice of the Commission president and a clearer and more open institutional structure. Parliament also called for some extension of the Union's competences. A majority in the Reflection Group supported Parliament's aspirations.

Participation in the Reflection Group enabled Parliament to influence the early thinking of governments. However, it was no substitute for partici-pating in the IGC itself, which would represent a significant stage in developing the constitutional framework of the Union. Parliament had high hopes that the precedent of the Reflection Group would allow it to attend the IGC on the same basis as the Commission: while the negotiations are among governments, the Commission, like the other participants, sits at the table, makes proposals and submits amendments, although it cannot veto the final outcome.

The issue was resolved at the European Council meeting in March 1996 where all save the French and British governments accepted Parliament's participation. However, the French and British opposition would not be moved and a compromise was found. It had been agreed that the IGC would work at two levels: monthly meetings of the foreign ministers to supervise and decide on key issues, and weekly meetings of an IGC working group, to which most governments nominated either their European affairs minister or their permanent representative. It was agreed that Parliament would nominate two representatives (it again chose Guigou and Brok) to the working group, but they would not attend all the meetings: only one per month. It was also agreed that meetings at the level of foreign ministers would begin with a discussion with the president of the European Parliament, Klaus Hänsch, accompanied by Brok and Guigou.

In practice, these arrangements enabled Parliament's representatives to be fully aware of what was happening in the IGC and to discuss every issue with the working group. They received all the IGC documents, could table their own documents and amendments, and participated in informal meetings such as dinners. They were thus able to play a full part in the IGC, despite not attending every meeting.

Already in the Reflection Group, but especially as the IGC proceeded, a general consensus emerged among most of the participants, including on the issues pressed by the European Parliament. But this consensus did not include the British government and it was clear that agreement would not be reached before the British elections in May 1997, just six weeks before the IGC was due to end. It was thus important to keep the British opposition party – and likely new government – very fully informed, and the Parliament's representatives in the IGC, with their access to documents, played a significant part in this (via their adviser, who was a Labour Party member). Labour MEPs were influential in the working group chaired by the party leader, Tony Blair, and including leading shadow ministers, which prepared the Labour Party's position on the IGC. The resulting report, endorsed unanimously by the party conference in 1995, came close to the Parliament's policy on issues such as co-decision, the Social Chapter and the Employment Chapter. In the six weeks between the election of the Labour government and the meeting of the European Council in Amsterdam in June 1997, this new British appproach facilitated agreement on such matters and hence on the Amsterdam Treaty.

The Amsterdam Treaty responded to a number of the Parliament's wishes. In addition to a certain strengthening of the Union's competences, for example in the new Employment Chapter, it took modest but significant steps of institutional reform. Thus it extended the co-decision procedure from 15 to 38 and eventually 40 articles, accounting for most of the non-agricultural legislation. It strengthened Parliament's role in co-decision through procedural changes, including elimination of the possibility for Council to adopt a text unilaterally if there is no agreement in the conciliation committee. It turned Parliament's vote on the president-designate of the Commission from a consultative one to a full legal confirmation and gave the president the right to approve the choice of the other commissioners. It extended somewhat the field of application of qualified majority voting, obliged the Council to publish the results of votes and statements recorded in the minutes, and stipulated a general right of access to EU documents. These steps were far from enough to satisfy the Parliament; and the failure to reform the Council's voting arrangements to provide for effective decision-taking after enlargement to Central and Eastern Europe was widely criticised. But the treaty did represent a further step in the process of incremental reinforcement of the federal characteristics of the Union, and in particular of movement towards a bicameral Europan legislature; and the Parliament again played a significant role in this stage of the Union's constitutional development.

Thus three major treaty revisions since Parliament became directly elected, the Single Act, the Treaty of Maastricht and the Treaty of Amsterdam, all came about in part because of pressure from the European Parliament. These episodes show how Parliament, though often frustrated, can act as a catalyst and stimulate change. Parliament embarked on its draft treaty project at a time of crisis in the Community, when confidence in its future was at an all-time low. Summits had broken down on the issue of budgetary contributions of member-states, the European economy was in a period of 'Euro-sclerosis' and few thought that there was any realistic chance of amending the treaties. Yet in thrashing out an agreement among the political groups in Parliament and pressing for support at various levels, Parliament was able to create a sufficient political momentum for at least some member-states' governments to press its case, and a majority of them to accept that there was a case to examine. The requirement of unanimity among the member-states for amending the treaties set limits to what could be achieved, but the momentum was enough to enable a compromise package to get through. Similarly there can be little doubt that in 1989–92 a number of the new treaty provisions, including those on extending the European Parliament's own powers, would not have found their way into the Treaty of Maastricht had it not been for the constant pressure by the Parliament; and the same is true of the Treaty of Amsterdam.

The process of stepwise development, from the Community's founding treaties onwards, has taken the European Parliament a long way from its origin as a largely consultative assembly. It has equal power, if not more, with the Council over almost all the non-agricultural expenditure of the European budget and some power over the rest. Co-decision has made it equal to the Council for some half of legislation. It has the power of assent over the Community's international treaties and the Union's acts of accession. It has the power of approval and of dismissal together with important means of control over the Commission. Since the procedure of qualified majority voting applies in the Council to most Community legislation, these two representative institutions have traversed a good part of the way towards becoming the two chambers of a federal legislature for the Community, while the Court of Justice ensures the rule of law. The Community has most of the economic powers that are usually required by a federal state, though the Union's other two 'pillars' lack effective powers with respect to internal and external security. While the federal state that Spinelli saw as being foreshadowed by the ECSC will not come about unless, and until, the Union has real powers in the field of security, the institutions already possess largely federal form and powers in the fields of the economy and the environment. With the completion of the single currency project, and majority voting as the general procedure in the Council in co-decision with the Parliament, the Community might be called, not a federal state, but at least a union of federal type.

Such an outcome is not, of course, assured. The process of integration could come to a halt or even go into reverse, particularly if further enlargement is not accompanied by strengthening of the institutions. But the process outlined in this chapter has gone remarkably far towards the end-product of European parliamentary government envisaged by Spinelli and the federalists. The fact of interdependence among European states has motivated the process of integration. The more dynamic economic actors have pressed for the economic integration, while France, Germany and their neighbours have sought to consolidate their security in the safe anchorage of the European institutions. But the increasingly parliamentary form of these institutions derives from the historic development of representative government and the rule of law, in which some of the most seminal moments have been recorded in the preceding chapters; and the Parliament's use of its power of dismissal to force the resignation of the Commission in March 1999 may also come to be seen as a seminal moment in the development of European parliamentary democracy.

The federal principle pioneered by the American Founding Fathers has exerted great influence, as has the example of Britain's parliamentary tradition. While France has taken many of the initiatives for integration, the German commitment to federal democracy has been decisive in promoting the development of the Community and Union, and of its Parliament in particular. The Dutch and the Belgians have contributed very significantly in the same direction. Italians, inspired by Spinelli's ideas with their roots in anglo-saxon political thought, have made a notable contribution. British MEPs too have made their mark on the development of the Parliament, often against the thrust of the British government policy deployed in the opposite direction. It may be hoped, however, that the British more generally are coming to see parliamentary democracy, which they did so much to develop, as a principle that is also applicable beyond the confines of the nation-state.

9 Foundations for Democracy in the European Union

John Pinder

Preceding chapters have presented a series of discrete stages in the development of liberal democracy, from pre-democratic institutions in the cities and provinces of the Low Countries, through the establishment of parliamentary government in England, to representative government based on popular sovereignty in the US and, as a striking example of its subsequent extension to many other countries, in postwar Germany. Two other themes, relating to possible further stages of democratic development, have also been considered: a more participatory form of democracy, and democracy beyond the nation-state. This concluding chapter seeks to place the successive stages in a historical perspective of the development from 'pre-democratic' to democratic institutions and, in particular, to consider their relationship with the two 'democratic transformations': to the level of the nation-state and, potentially, to the level of a union of nation-states.[1]

Self-government in the Low Countries

Two constellations of wealthy cities emerged from mediaeval Europe: in northern Italy and in the Low Countries. The merchants and artisans of such cities showed themselves well able to develop pre-democratic institutions. But the bitter rivalries among the Italian city-states led most of them to succumb, first to despots who were deemed better able to conduct their wars, then to imperial powers against which the jealously independent cities proved incapable of joining forces. Those of the Low Countries, however, achieved a good measure of self-government under the protection of the Burgundian dukedom. The citizens were left to look after their own affairs in return for their financial support for the dukes' wider concerns, particularly external and military affairs.

Chapter 2 shows how a variety of pre-democratic structures evolved as the Flemish cities moved from the Middle Ages into the more open society of the Renaissance. The rule of law came increasingly to apply to the actions of public authorities as well as to the citizens. Concepts of citizens' rights became established, among them the principle of government by consent. While there was no formal participation by the citizens as a whole, there were informal assemblies in public places. Formally, the precursors of representative institutions grew in importance: the Estates of the nobility, the clergy and the burgesses, with the composition of the latter becoming based on a process of selection of representatives of the crafts and corporations. By the twelfth century legislative procedures had begun to replace custom as the source of law. The idea surfaced of a contract between prince and people in the confirmation in office of the heir to the local count's authority. A concept of provincial autonomy had existed in the public law of the Low Countries since the Middle Ages and the constitutions, courts and customs of the provinces and cities were respected. There was what Van Caenegem calls a sort of 'federal monarchy', with the central institutions having their own political, judicial, legal and financial functions, and above all their responsibility for security, while the cities and provinces ran their own local affairs.

Into this comfortable and progressive state of affairs, sixteenth-century absolutism in the form of the Spanish autocracy intruded like, as Van Caenegem puts it, 'a sudden and icy blast'. The Flemish lost their autonomy and hence, for over three centuries, their chance to contribute to the further development of democracy. But crucially for that development, the Dutch proved able to resist.

The northern provinces of the Low Countries had shared with the Flemish in the development of pre-democratic institutions. But unlike the Flemish they were able, joined together as the seven United Provinces, to defend the traditions and freedoms that they believed Philip II had no right to disturb: freedom of conscience as against religious intolerance; the rule of law against arbitrary personal rule; local autonomy against imperial autocracy; and, eventually, a republic against an absolutist monarch. In 1581 the States General, the assembly of the United Provinces, approved the Act of Abjuration, enjoining their citizens not to obey Philip on the ground that he was a tyrant who had forfeited his sovereignty. They did not seek to construct a new state, but looked instead for a new monarch: in effect for a constitutional monarch. They drew up treaties to explain to potential monarchs the conditions attached to the post, embodying the principle enunciated in the Act of Abjuration, that 'the subjects are not created for the benefit of the prince . . . but that the prince is created for the subjects.'

It was only because none of the existing European monarchs seemed willing to accept their conditions that the Dutch established their Republic; and instead of a crowned head of state, each of the provinces appointed a stadholder. Most of the provinces, including the most important ones, appointed only successive Princes of Orange as stadholders, given the prestige that Willem I ('the Silent') had conferred on that House in leading the revolt against Philip; and the stadholders were accorded some sovereign rights, including the power to make a number of appointments and, usually, the posts of the union's captain-general and admiral-general. Thus they could play a leading part in the affairs of the United Provinces. But there was no question that the States, as the city and provincial councils were called, would tolerate any form of absolute personal rule.

The States were not elected representative assemblies in the modern sense. Their members were almost all wealthy burghers, selected by a process of cooptation from among the cities' commercial patricians, or 'regents'. But such bodies can be seen as pre-democratic institutions, in which, in contrast to autocratic personal rule, all members of an association are held to be 'adequately qualified to participate on an equal footing with the others in the process of governing the association'.[2] Although the category of burghers from which the members of the States were drawn was narrow, the success of the Dutch Republic demonstrated, as Kossmann observes in Chapter 3, that a non-absolutist form of government worked better than absolute monarchy, and that political freedom, combined with religious and economic freedom, had liberated the dynamic energies of the Dutch, in art, commerce, society and politics, as nowhere else in Europe. The Dutch system was to prove a solid foundation for a new philosophy of liberal government.

United, moreover, the seven provinces had been strong enough to defend themselves against the power of Spain. Not that the institutions of the union were themselves strong. The seven provinces had one vote each in the States General and unanimity was, in theory, required for binding decisions. Nor was there a federal administration. But decisions on foreign policy, defence, and the tax to pay for these were, given a sufficient majority, in practice carried out, in no small part because the province of Holland, which as the largest and richest paid three-fifths of the total tax, acted as an enlightened hegemon, giving the others influence out of proportion to the size of their contributions, and thus securing agreement to an effective unified policy.

The stadholder, as commander of the armed forces, also participated in the design and execution of foreign policy and defence and could thus help to hold the United Provinces to an effective common policy. But, since he was appointed by the States of the provinces and could obtain no finance for his actions without their consent, he had to comply with their wishes and, above all, could never cross the will of the regents of Holland. Thus the Dutch Republic was not only a confederacy that fought off Philip II and whose provinces had pronounced liberal elements. It also produced a prince who had to work with pre-democratic assemblies and was thus capable of making a deal with the English Parliament and initiating the crucial next stage in the development of liberal democracy.

Britain: to constitutional monarchy and parliamentary government

Stadholder Willem III and the United Provinces were, by the late 1680s, confronted by the expansionist hegemony of Louis XIV of France. The Dutch feared they might lose their trade, shipping and even independence. With a population not much more than one-tenth that of France, they sought to avoid at all costs a hostile alliance of the English and the French, such as had attacked the Netherlands in 1672 when Charles II was king. On the contrary, Willem and the Dutch needed England as an ally against France. But this would not be possible while Charles's successor, the Catholic James II, was on the throne, with the Tories sympathetic to his absolutist pretensions.

England was, indeed, divided like Europe, with the Whigs ranged against the Tory supporters of divine right. The Whigs believed, on the contrary, in authority derived from the people's consent and in constitutional arrangements to ensure that this was so. They were impressed by the Dutch example and by the political philosophy of John Locke, himself influenced by his lengthy sojourn in Holland. They were the obvious partners for the Dutch, who were convinced that absolute monarchy was a 'corrupted and exceedingly dangerous form of government'.[3] The Dutch judged rightly that, with support for James weakened through his actions in undermining Parliament and the judiciary and through his commitment to Catholicism, an intervention with sufficient force would succeed in ousting him and turning the system round in the direction they and the Whigs preferred. The States therefore agreed to make the vast investment that Willem needed to launch a fleet of 500 ships to convey to England some 6000 horses and over 20,000 men.

In order to secure enough backing from political forces in England and hence to make a deal with Parliament, Willem undertook, in communications to both Parliament and the public, to restore the rights and liberties of Englishmen that James had ignored; and he promised that England would be governed by 'the joint concurrence of King and Parliament' and that the levying of money for the crown without a 'grant of Parliament' would be illegal.[4] British support for him was not so strong as Whig historians have claimed. But shrewd men in the States who had to foot the bill judged it strong enough to tip the scales, not just for the immediate future but also for the longer term; and they were proved right in the event. Despite their instinctive revulsion against the deposition of a king, many Tories had been upset by James's Catholicism and by his behaviour towards Parliament and the courts; the Whigs were no mean party; and people as well as Parliament came to appreciate the growth of parliamentary power that followed what the Whigs were to call the Glorious Revolution, so that the virtually bloodless revolution was not reversed.

Thus Willem III of the Netherlands struck his bargain with Parliament, including the Bill of Rights and Parliament's crucial budgetary powers, and so became the constitutional monarch, William III of England: of a realm that was soon to be extended, through the Union with Scotland, to Great Britain and, a century later, to the United Kingdom. His character was of autocratic stamp and he was inclined to exploit his royal powers to the extent possible. But he was constrained by the need to retain credibility not only among the British but also with the Dutch States. His commitments to Parliament and to the 'liberties of Englishmen' had to be made both very publicly and rapidly, in order to secure his position when he displaced James and to obtain the resources he needed for the war against France; and those commitments had to be sustained, at least enough to maintain Parliament's essential powers, in order to ensure continued support not only in England but also in the United Provinces: both essential for the success of his project of resistance to the hegemony of absolutist France. As an experienced stadholder, his skills included those required to deal with difficult and sovereign assemblies; and even if he had been tempted to depart from the role of constitutional monarch, it was quite clear that the States would never tolerate any pretensions to absolutism in his role as king of England.

It is ironic that, while William was uniquely qualified to play his part in creating the constitutional monarchy and the parliamentary form of government, it was also his growing unpopularity in England which consolidated that system through the 1690s. He continued to need money for the war until it ended in 1697 and the taxes that resulted were highly unpopular. Although Parliament approved them, it was perceived to do so reluctantly and to the minimum necessary. So its popularity grew as that of the king declined; and parliamentary government became solidly established.

Thus the Glorious Revolution which, as Israel affirms in Chapter 4, was made possible by the Dutch intervention, was a fundamental event in the development of British democracy. In place of a would-be absolutist monarchy, England, and soon Great Britain as a whole, became a constitutionalist kingdom: what Israel has called a 'crowned republic'.[5] From the most unstable, divided, revolution-prone country in seventeenth-century Europe it became one of the most stable and united in the eighteenth century. Against the expectations of many in Europe that a parliamentary regime would be spendthrift and ineffectual, it proved effective and successful enough to emerge victorious from the War of Succession – thanks, ironically again, in no small part to the fiscal and financial regime installed by William III, with its taxable capacity and the Bank of England. The system was not yet democratic in the extent of the electorate. But Parliament, not the monarch, became the institution that enacted the laws and the dominant partner in government. The pre-democratic institutions were far enough advanced to provide the basis for the subsequent development of democracy, showing how 'ancient pluralism' with its initially narrow circles of elites can, through a process of 'conflict and accommodation, broaden gradually over wider social strata', and thus evolve to become a stable democratic regime.[6]

The significance of this transition to parliamentary government was not confined to the British. Far from it. What Dahl has called the 'first democratic transformation', to direct participation by citizens of a city-state, which occurred in Athens in the fifth century BC, was now to be followed by the 'second democratic transformation', to representative government of a nation-state. The idea of democracy was thereby transferred from the city-state 'to the much larger scale of the nation-state'; and 'theoretical barriers' to extending the scale of the democratic polity were removed. Important problems which could 'never be solved within the narrow limits of a city state', and which grew 'ever more numerous as interdependence increased', could be dealt with 'more effectively over a far larger territory', so that the 'capacity of citizens to govern themselves was greatly enhanced'.[7]

The launching in England of this second democratic transformation had 'an immense impact on Europe as a whole'.[8] It enabled William to achieve his aim of preventing an absolutist hegemony in Europe: an example that Britain was able to replicate at critical junctures in subsequent European history. In the German states it strengthened the constitutional traditions against absolutist pretensions. The political philosopher Samuel Pufendorf was greatly impressed.[9] In France, Montesquieu and Voltaire were to take the British constitutional monarchy as a model, as were many in the first stages of the French Revolution. Across the Atlantic, New Englanders had overthrown James's administration by the force of their own arms and the idea of armed resistance to a tyrannical government took root, with profound consequences for the further development of democracy.[10]

The US: to popular sovereignty and federal government

In their resistance to the colonial policy of George III and Lord North, the Americans invoked the 'rights of Englishmen', or of all British subjects, referring to the common law and notably to the rights and liberties of the 1689 Bill of Rights. The prevalent political philosophy among the Founding Fathers was that of Locke, mediated in part through Montesquieu; and Hume had a particular influence on Alexander Hamilton and James Madison. Most of the delegates at the Philadelphia Convention sought a constitution patterned, as Bonwick puts it in Chapter 5, 'as closely as circumstances would permit, after the English Constitution'.

Americans were also much influenced by British radicals such as Tom Paine, whose works were to have a great impact in Britain and in France as well.[11] The idea of popular sovereignty had a special resonance, appealing to the Puritan tradition among others and offering an antithesis to the arbitrary monarchical rule that applied in the colonies. Reacting against excessive concentration of power, the Americans also rejected parliamentary sovereignty, preferring that power be distributed as far as possible among different institutions.

Many Americans were for similar reasons reluctant to establish a powerful central government and wished to continue under the limited union of the Articles of Confederation. A few, notably Alexander Hamilton, mindful of the difficulty of fighting the War of Independence as 13 separate states, and subsequently of the failure of the weak confederal system to deal satisfactorily with their common problems and with the quarrels among them, wanted a unitary American state whose institutions would replace those of the several existing states. Many, perhaps a majority, desired a rebalanced federal system that would erect a stronger central government, but nevertheless respect the states as major sources of political authority. The combination of these two concerns, both valid, was the federal constitution, dividing the powers between the federal and the state levels of government. The main powers of the federal government were to be in the fields of foreign affairs and defence, internal and external trade, currency, and tax to pay for the exercise of these functions. The states' governments were to deal with everything not allocated to the centre, which meant most of the day-to-day process of governing. The institutions at both levels were to be based on the rule of law, representative government and popular sovereignty.

Just as, a century earlier, the transition of England to constitutional monarchy and parliamentary sovereignty had wide-ranging significance in Europe and America, so the US constitution had significance far beyond the time and place of its creation. What was remotely implicit in British constitutional doctrine as expounded by Blackstone became directly explicit in the United States. Americans rejected British attempts to apply parliamentary sovereignty to them, but effectively extended and transformed the principle of authority exercised through representative institutions into the more fundamental yet functional principle of a sovereign people as the only source of legitimate government, and then adapted it to the requirements of a complex society by constructing a carefully articulated federal system. Popular sovereignty was an immensely powerful concept; the 'rights of Englishmen' were translated into the rights of all men; and, if representative government could be said to have removed the theoretical barrier to extending the scale of the democratic polity, federal government showed a good way of doing so in practice, without making the functions of government as a whole too remote from the citizens. As Acton was to put it, the federal idea could be seen as 'completing the principles of a liberal constitution in a way that was capable of unlimited extension'.[12] With the advance of interdependence among modern states, it would, Dahl has suggested, become possible to envisage 'something like the second transformation writ large on a world scale': that is, a 'third transformation', taking the system of representative government from the level of the nation-state to a wider, multinational polity;[13] and if the 'world scale' of which Dahl writes is beyond the scope of this book, the European scale is highly relevant to it. As Bonwick puts it in the last sentence of his chapter, the Americans at least were 'convinced that their actions had universal as well as domestic importance, and hoped their experience would be helpful to Europeans'.

France: Proudhon and decentralist federalism

In the first phase of the French Revolution, almost all the revolutionaries wanted a constitutional monarchy respecting civil liberties, after the British pattern. Most members of the Constituent Assembly looked to Britain and, above all, to the United States. The federal idea of unity in diversity prevailed at the great gathering of delegations at the Champ de Mars celebrating the first anniversary of the storming of the Bastille; and the Girondins, who were until 1792 the leading party in the assembly, held to that idea until they were eliminated by the Jacobins. After the king was deposed, a significant group wanted a federal constitution following the American example. As Tocqueville was to observe, however, the US Constitution was based on a very strong civil society. But the absolutist principle espoused by French kings had inhibited the emergence of a civil society strong enough to sustain a democratic government through the strains of revolution and war; and those who had been influenced by Britain and America were thrust aside by the Jacobins.

The Jacobins were intransigent centralisers. They saw the federalists as subverting the 'Republic, one and indivisible'. They followed Rousseau's dictum, cited by Voyenne in Chapter 6, that the social contract 'gives the body politic an absolute power' over all its members; and this led to the Terror, to which the reaction was Napoleon's dictatorial regime. Republican France reverted to the centralist state tradition of the kings, mixed with a powerful dose of nationalism.

Jacobin centralism has been a recurrent theme in France since the revolution. It was, however, soon opposed by liberals such as Tocqueville and Constant, looking to the American and British examples and building on Locke and Montesquieu. From the left came an original French variety of anti-jacobinism: that of Pierre-Joseph Proudhon, which strongly influenced workers and their organisations from the mid-nineteenth century up to World War One and has continued to provide inspiration for the personalist movement. His work is also very relevant to contemporary radical political philosophy that stresses participation and active citizenship, and in particular to what Held has called 'the model of democratic autonomy'.[14]

Proudhon is most widely known for his slogan, 'property is theft'. He liked bold phrases; and that one he coined in his first work, written at the age of 21 after a rapid process of self-education. It is not so well known that, after mature reflection, he came to see property as an essential defence of freedom. He opposed collectivisation, which he regarded as leading to tyranny, but he was also against an absolute right to property, holding that inequality of ownership caused what would now be called a structural imbalance in society, whereas with inequality reduced, economic life could be based on freely negotiated mutual agreements between equal partners.

If his initial slogan for economics was 'property is theft', for politics it was 'government is oppression'. Just as he came to regard property as a bulwark of liberty, however, so he was to see the need for government even after the excessive inequalities that made for oppression had been removed – unlike marxists who persisted in supposing that the state would wither away. But he remained firmly opposed to the jacobin concept of the state and to the strands in Rousseau's thinking that led towards it.

After the turbulence of 1848–49, he reached a conclusion that pleased neither left nor right: that liberty and equality should be 'brought together in the scales of Justice'. Thus he accepted the merits of the state, if its function was to guarantee justice – or, in modern parlance, if there were to be economic and social as well as political rights. He now saw liberty and authority as complementary poles, with society developing through the tension between them.

This led Proudhon to a form of federalism in its widest sense, economic and social as well as political. Politically, he laid stress on states' rights and the principle of self-government or, in the contemporary jargon, subsidiarity. But he differed from the Swiss and American understanding of federalism when he applied it also to the organisation of society, and in particular to economic 'mutuality', with reciprocity of services rendered.

Although radical political writers in English have not, since Laski,[15] shown much interest in Proudhon's thought, it could make a valuable contribution to contemporary thinking about participatory citizenship and democratic autonomy. While accepting the necessity of the classic civil rights, Held argues that they are not sufficient: that citizens should also enjoy the conditions for effective participation and that public policy should help make this possible by seeking to remove structural causes of inequality, such as asymmetries of power between classes, races, men and women, politicians and 'ordinary citizens'. Particularly close to Proudhon's federalism is the stress on participation in local government and in economic and social organisations.[16]

Politically, Proudhon saw federalism as the antithesis of jacobin centralism. Proudhonian personalists are firm advocates of decentralisation in France. But they have also been among the pioneers of the European idea, combining their insistence on the need for local autonomy with acceptance that a minimum of central federal power is also required: in contemporary jargon, the principle of subsidiarity.

Germany: a federal democracy in a uniting Europe

German enthusiasm for liberal constitutional principles was already demonstrated in Pufendorf's reaction to the Glorious Revolution. By 1848, the drafters of a German constitution in the assembly that met in the Paulskirche in Frankfurt showed a solid commitment to those principles. But they were not strong enough to overcome the autocratic resistance of the Prussian monarch. Germany was to be unified by Bismarck on more authoritarian lines. Proudhon, as Voyenne shows, foresaw that the centralist structure of the unified Germany would lead to conflict among the European powers, even if he may not have envisaged the scale of the disasters that ensued, from World War One, through the rise of Hitler, to the catastrophe of World War Two. By 1945, the German polity was a tabula rasa. But there was an old tradition of pluralism, with federal elements, as well as of liberal thinking on which to build.

Among the four occupying powers, the Soviet Union was bent on establishing a Soviet state, if not in Germany as a whole, then in its eastern zone of occupation. France, following its wartime experiences, was not in a strong position. So it was up to the Americans and the British to stand for the principles of liberal democracy.

The first task of the Allies was to root out the Nazis from positions where they could pollute the postwar German polity. This was, as Glees shows in Chapter 7, rapidly and sufficiently well accomplished. At the same time the people had to be fed, education recommenced and reconstruction set in train. The Americans were determined to ensure the installation of a market economy, which they saw as a necessary condition of pluralist democracy; and they ensured the success of the currency reform that laid the basis for the future strength of the Deutschmark. The Americans also provided Marshall Aid for Germany as well as other West European countries and, together with the British, kept the western part of Berlin free from Soviet domination by a sustained and costly airlift of food and other supplies. All this effort on the part of the Allies laid a foundation of stability and growing prosperity on which German democracy could flourish and helped to convince Germans that they should cooperate and integrate with western democracies.

The Americans and British moved as fast as they could to ensure that democratic German institutions were established. Governments were created in the Länder of their occupation zones before the end of 1945 and local elections held early in 1946. Democratic political parties were revived; and the British in particular were successful in helping to set up free trade unions and independent newspapers, and in influencing the development of local government. But it was not possible to create all-German political institutions, because although the four powers had agreed that this should be done jointly for all four zones, the western Allies were unable to reach agreement about it with the Soviet Union, which refused to countenance the institutions of liberal democracy. It was only in the spring of 1948, following the communist coup in Prague, that the Americans, British and French decided a West German state must be established; and they told the ministers-president of the Länder in their zones to convene an assembly to produce a constitution within a year. The Parliamentary Council, as the assembly was called, was composed of representatives of the democratic political parties.

The aim of the French was a loose confederation of Länder without a central power strong enough to present any possible future danger to France. The British envisaged a quite centralised federal system. The Americans wanted a federal system on the pattern of the United States. Already in November 1947 General Clay, the military governor of the American zone, had sent a memorandum to the ministers-president on the need for a democratic federal constitution for Germany. Konrad Adenauer and the Christian Democrats accepted the principle of an American-style federal system, while the Social Democratic Party, like the British Labour government, preferred greater centralisation. In the event, the draft of the Constitutional Assembly was closer to the American model, with modifications that stemmed from German experience. Instead of a senate, there was to be the Bundesrat, comprising representatives of the Land governments. The legislative role of the federal parliament covered a wider field than that of the US Congress, but the Länder had more responsibility than American states for executing federal policies. The federal executive was to be a government responsible to the legislature, following the British example, rather than a directly elected president as in the US. On receiving the draft, the Allied military governors raised a number of objections, following which the assembly made some changes. But it was essentially the German draft that emerged as the Basic Law.

The Federal Republic's Constitution, for that is what the Basic Law became, was the work of German politicians. But the western Allies had insisted, as Glees underlines in Chapter 7, that it must be based on the principles of liberal democracy, including fundamental rights; and the Americans in particular emphasised the need for a federal structure. The Allies had also ensured that it would be drafted by representatives of democratic parties. So the constitution was profoundly influenced by those principles, and in particular by liberal democracy in the tradition established by the British and the Americans. The German drafters produced a thoroughly sound constitution along these lines, not because of specific interventions by the Allies, but because they and the postwar political class they represented, which the Allies had made sure was to replace the apparatus of Nazi rule, were themselves convinced that this was the better way. Had it been otherwise, the result would not have endured. Despite all the differences of circumstance, there is an interesting parallel with the way in which parliamentary government and constitutional monarchy took root in Britain after the intervention of the Dutch.

It can hardly be denied that the outcome has been a great success. Germany, having accepted the Anglo-American tradition, has become a solidly based democracy and a pillar of the Atlantic Alliance and the European Union – the latter, thanks largely to the partnership offered by the French and warmly welcomed by the Germans, which has led the uniting of Europe during the past half-century.

DEMOCRACY BEYOND THE NATION-STATE

The story so far concerns the 'second democratic transformation', starting from the pre-democratic institutions of cities of the Renaissance and ending with the liberal democracies of the modern nation-state: from the Flemish cities, through the Dutch Republic, the British constitutional monarchy, the federal democracy of the United States, and French traditions of democratic thought, to the establishment of the postwar Federal Republic of Germany. Postwar Austria has, with local variations, followed a course similar to that of Germany. Italy, whose first national constitution following the Risorgimento was based on British political principles, likewise adopted a liberal democratic constitution after World War Two. A similar form of democracy has since become consolidated in Greece, Portugal and Spain; and adding these to the established democracies of the Low Countries, the Scandinavians and the Swiss, liberal democracy has been extended to all the states of Western Europe. Most of the states of Central and Eastern Europe have, since the fall of the Soviet empire, been moving in that direction, and some have already arrived. Beyond Europe, the old democracies of North America and Australasia have, since the war, been joined by India, Japan and a number of smaller states; democracy has gained ground in Latin America; and pre-democratic institutions are to be seen, at stages more or less advanced, in many other states.

The second democratic transformation has made great strides in the second half of the twentieth century. But while the principles of liberal democracy have thus been vindicated, those who support them should not be complacent. Many emergent democracies in Eastern Europe, Latin America and elsewhere are not yet solidly based. Many established democracies have to adapt to the pressures for improved performance, together with government closer to the people for which, in Europe, the German and Swiss federal systems and the proudhonian federalist thought outlined in Chapter 5 are particularly suggestive. Beyond that, there is the impact of transnational forces on the institutions of the nation-state raising the question whether, as Dahl suggests, a 'third democratic transformation' is 'now within reach':[17] whether the democratic institutions of the nation-state are to be complemented by democratic institutions of groups of states, designed to deal with their common problems. While the group for which this question is most actual, the European Union, is now concerned mainly with its citizens' common economic and environmental problems, its origins lay in the grim reality of the conflicts inherent in the 'Westphalian model of state sovereignty'.[18]

The European Union and its pre-democratic institutions

The European Community was created following the catastrophic climax of that Westphalian system in World War Two. The principal aim was, as the Schuman Declaration that in 1950 launched the establishment of the Community put it, to eliminate 'the age-old opposition between France and Germany' so that any war between the two would become 'not merely unthinkable but materially impossible'.[19] This was to be done by placing the coal and steel sectors, then the industrial basis for war potential, under the control of common institutions with effective common policy instruments: in effect by setting up the pre-democratic institutions of what amounted to a joint system of government for those sectors of the economies of the founding member-states, France, Germany, Italy and the Benelux countries. Jean Monnet, who initiated the Declaration and was responsible for drafting it, saw this as 'a first step in the federation of Europe', to be built through successive 'concrete achievements'. Thus he envisaged what may be called a series of pre-federal steps, which would include the grant of specific powers to pre-democratic European institutions. Just as pre-democratic institutions do not necessarily lead to liberal democracy, so the pre-federal powers and institutions do not necessarily lead to a federal system. But it was the clear intention of Monnet and others among the founders that they should.

Monnet, in his inaugural speech as the first president of the High Authority, as the executive of the European Coal and Steel Community was called, expounded the pre-democratic and pre-federal elements in the institutions. The High Authority was to exercise its executive powers direct to legal persons, not through the administrations of the member-states. Its acts were subject to the rule of Community law, judged by an independent Court of Justice. It was responsible to a Common Assembly; and although the powers of what was later to become the European Parliament were then very limited, the treaty provided that it would eventually be directly elected by the citizens, clearly implying that it should be endowed with real, usable powers, and thus pointing towards a system of representative government for the Community.[20]

While Monnet, who was the prime influence in the launching of the Community, was not much concerned about constitutions as such, he had great respect for the American federal system. One of his close collaborators affirmed that *The Federalist* of Hamilton, Jay and Madison was 'the Missal of his faith' and another observed that it was always on his desk.[21] Altiero Spinelli, who worked with Monnet to write that speech,[22] and who was also to leave his mark on the process of uniting Europe, was likewise, as Corbett points out in Chapter 8, profoundly influenced by 'the great American political experience' and by the British writers on federalism, themselves steeped in the British tradition of liberal democracy.[23] He in turn was to influence not only the federalist movement but also Italian policy towards Europe: for example, when Italy insisted that the concept of a European army, for which the member-states of the ECSC in the early 1950s drew up the treaty for a European Defence Community, could not be valid without democratic federal institutions to which it would be responsible; and when Prime Minister De Gasperi consequently initiated the proposal that the Common Assembly draft the Treaty for a European Political Community, which provided for institutions along those lines.[24] But that fell by the wayside when the French Assemblée Nationale failed to ratify the EDC treaty. So, unable to make the leap to a federal state, the Community continued to develop in the way Monnet had foreseen, adding elements of pre-federal institutions, powers and instruments to the initial basis of the Community, partly through developments within the framework of the treaties as they stood and partly through new treaties, such as the Treaty establishing the European Economic Community, and amending treaties of which the most notable have been the Single European Act, the Maastricht Treaty of European Union, and the Treaty of Amsterdam.

Steps towards a European democracy

The treaties, which were in themselves law and which also provided for a process of legislation by the Community institutions, stipulated that the Court of Justice must ensure 'that the law is observed'.[25] In carrying out this duty, the Court has ensured that Community law is applied direct to citizens and other legal persons, to the point where the Community, with respect to its legal system, 'possesses most of the characteristics of a federation'.[26] Although there was not, until the Maastricht and Amsterdam Treaties, any treaty provision regarding citizens' rights, the Court also held that it could not fulfil its duty unless fundamental rights and freedoms were respected in the acts of the Community institutions, since the member-states, being democracies based on respect for such rights, could not be expected to accept the application of Community law unless the rights were upheld. Thus the Community has developed, within its fields of competence which are largely economic and environmental, an effective rule of law based on fundamental rights: one of the essential pillars of liberal democracy.

A twin pillar is representative government; and here the Community remains pre-democratic.

The Commission, as the executive institution, has certain attributes of a government. It initiates legislation and is responsible for the execution after enactment. But it is still closely constrained by the Council of Ministers, representing the executives of the member-states.

The Council constrains the Commission both by itself taking detailed decisions on executive matters and through a network of committees of officials responsible to the member-states' ministers. But its primary function is legislative. It alone enacts the laws in fields that, following the Maastricht and Amsterdam treaties, still account for about half of the Community's legislation and it plays a dominant part in determining about half of the budget, principally the agricultural expenditure. For some of the legislative decisions the unanimity procedure, which favours inter-governmental negotiation rather than parliamentary procedures, applies. But most of them can be taken by a qualified majority of some seventy per cent of the weighted votes. The Council is usually composed of elected ministers responsible, in their national governments, for the subject in question, as is also the Bundesrat, Germany's 'house of the states', which is composed of ministers of the Länder. But such indirect representation leaves the link with the citizens weak.[27] Unless it is complemented by a directly elected house of the citizens with at least equal legislative power, the Council will remain a pre-democratic institution rather than the states' house in a democratic federal system.

The European Parliament and its powers

The legislature of such a system should have a double legitimacy, with the member-states represented in the states' house and the house of the people representing the citizens. The directly elected European Parliament is the institution designed to perform the latter function.[28] After 1688, the House of Commons demonstrated how a legislative chamber representing voters in this way could become the key institution that distinguished liberal democracy from other forms of government; and the United States carried the principle to a logical conclusion, followed by many other countries. Chapter 8 shows how the European Parliament has, with the support of a number of political parties, interest groups, Parliaments and governments, sought with some degree of success to strengthen its powers in order to fulfil that role, and thus to play its part in completing a 'third democratic trans-formation', carrying democracy from the level of the nation-state to that of a multinational union.

The Parliament declared its intention of securing that role when, following the first direct European elections in 1979, it designed and then, in 1984, approved its draft treaty establishing the European Union. This work was inspired by Spinelli, who saw it as the way to take a big step towards a federal Europe. The Parliament, led by Spinelli, proposed; but the governments and Parliaments of the member-states had the power to dispose. Corbett notes the support for the project, in particular from President Mitterrand and from Germany, Italy, Belgium and the Netherlands, together with a number of British MEPs who played a notable part in designing the draft treaty. But the British government was bent on defending Westminster's parliamentary sovereignty. Nor was Mitterrand enthusiastic about powers for the European Parliament. Since treaty amendment requires ratification by all the member-states, the British opposition, along with French doubts, was enough to stand in the way of the extension of its powers that the Parliament proposed.

The Parliament was nevertheless strengthened. By the mid-1980s there was growing concern that Europe was becoming less competitive within the world economy, and the fragmentation of the European market was seen as a significant cause. So the Commission's proposal to 'complete the single market' by 1992 through a vast programme of Community legislation was supported by the governments of most member-states. Most of them also wanted the legislative acts to be adopted by more effective and democratic procedures, and so supported institutional reforms such as more majority voting in the Council and greater powers for the European Parliament. The result was the Single European Act, in which commitment to the Commission's single market programme was accompanied by moves towards the institutional reforms proposed in the Parliament's draft treaty. Such a combination of new common instruments to deal with a particular problem, together with reforms designed to make the institutions that are to use the instruments more effective and democratic, has been a recurrent feature of the development of the Community's pre-democratic institutions.

The first instance was the establishment of the European Coal and Steel Community, with its institutional structure for governing the coal and steel industries of the member-states. A second example gave the Parliament significant budgetary powers, when the Dutch, true to the tradition that had controlled expenditure at the time of the stadholders, insisted that there should be no public expenditure by the Community without parliamentary approval; and since it would not be practicable for the parliaments of the several member-states to undertake this task, it would have to be done by the European Parliament. With support from the Germans, Italians and Belgians in particular, the Parliament was given equal power with the Council over fields of expenditure that now amount to over half the Community's budget.

The Single European Act followed, then the Maastricht and Amsterdam treaties, which provided for economic and monetary union and a further strengthening of the Parliament's powers. The French desire to regain a share in control over monetary policy, which had been lost in practice to the German Bundesbank, as well as to ensure that the reunited Germany would remain anchored in the Community system, supplied the essential impulse for the programme to establish the single currency and, in order to offer some satisfaction to the Germans, Italians, Belgians, Dutch and others who wanted to move farther towards parliamentary government, the co-decision procedure was also adopted, whereby laws must be approved by the Parliament as well as the Council; and this gives the Parliament legislative power equivalent to that of the Council in fields likely to account for half of all Community legislation. To that extent, the Parliament and Council together now approximate to a two-chamber federal legislature. Many of the Community's laws are, however, still enacted by the Council alone; and the 'pillars' that the Maastricht Treaty set up alongside the Community, giving the Union competences relating to internal and external security, remain predominantly inter-governmental. But the Maastricht and Amsterdam treaties also gave the Parliament the power to approve, or not, the appointment of, first, the President of each new Commission, then of the Commission as a whole; and this, together with the Parliament's power to dismiss it which induced the Commission's resignation in March 1999, has opened up a path that may lead to its becoming a European parliamentary executive.

A federal union and democratic autonomy?

The pre-democratic institutions of the European Community are, then, together with its pre-federal powers and instruments, fairly far advanced. There is a Court responsible for what amounts to a federal rule of law. There is, in the Commission, an executive with certain attributes of a responsible government, but which lacks adequate executive competences and a sufficiently clear democratic accountability. There is, in the European Parliament, a house of the people which has powers equivalent to those of the house of the states with respect to some half of the legislation and of the budget and to which the executive is in part accountable. The Council is a house of the states which votes by majority for most, though not all, legislation but which retains a role, executive as well as legislative, that is more predominant than is, for such an indirectly elected body, compatible with the principles of representative government. The main changes that would bring the institutions of the Community into line with those principles are reformist rather than revolutionary: completion of the Parliament's right of co-decision with the Council; generalisation of the majority voting procedure and open legislative sessions in the Council; fuller executive competences for the Commission and a more normal accountability to the legislature.

That applies to the Community, with its largely economic fields of competence. But the way in which the institutions work in the 'pillars' relating to internal and external security is much farther removed from the principles of rule of law and representative government, with the Court of Justice largely absent, the Commission's role consultative rather than executive, the Parliament's presence scarcely felt, and the unanimity procedure prevailing in the Council. Here, the process of combining the adoption of common instruments with the enhancement of democratic elements in the institutions has scarcely begun. While cooperation in cross-frontier aspects of security within the union may well be developed into integration, the integration of instruments of armed force on any major scale would amount to the creation of a federal state. If the Community completes the institutions of representative government in addition to the rule of law, it might appropriately be called a democratic federal union. But a federal state is another matter.

This raises the question of which comes first, a nation or a state? Van Caenegem observes in Chapter 2 that in the Low Countries the state came before the nation, whereas in England the nation came first. There appears to be no a priori answer. In the Community, as we have seen, there has been an iterative process between the development of institutions that represent the people, directly or indirectly, and the integration of instruments which, while not reaching into the armed force that is the hard core of sovereignty, are nevertheless part of the instrumentarium of a modern state. It seems reasonable to suppose that the capacity of citizens of a group of nations to sustain a democratic system to deal with their common problems may be developed by stages, as they become accustomed to pre-democratic institutions having responsibility for dealing with matters that are not the most central to sovereignty.

Without contesting that the institutions of liberal democracy, and in particular the rule of law and representative government, are necessary, those who argue for a more participatory form of democracy hold them to be insufficient; and it can in particular be argued that the development of enough solidarity to enable citizens to sustain a multinational democracy requires a common view of democracy that goes beyond the classical liberal model.

Information technology might make it physically possible to extend the direct democracy of a Greek city-state to the citizens of a large nation-state or even a multinational federation.[29] Less radically, IT can be used as an aid to liberal democracy, through more direct links between the citizens and their representatives; and more conventionally, such links can be strengthened by applying the principle of subsidiarity: decentralising to levels as close to the people as possible those functions of government that such levels can effectively perform. This concept can be derived from both American and German federalism; and Chapter 5 has shown how, contrary to the traditional centralism of the French state, it is intrinsic to proudhonian federalist thought. But both Proudhon and the contemporary argument for participatory democracy go deeper.

The essence of this argument is that, to participate fully in a democracy, citizens need to enjoy a degree of equality which is impeded by the structure of society, for example in the relationships between enterprises and employees or between rich and poor. In calling this 'democratic autonomy', Held shows an affinity with Proudhon's concern for equality as a basis for the autonomy of citizens and enterprises and local governments.[30] The main field for the application of such ideas would lie within the states of the European Union. But the ideas may be seen as relevant to the Union in two respects.

There is inequality in the structure of the Union because of the wide divergence between the economic levels of the member-states. The Union has its 'cohesion' policies to assist the development of the poorer states. But it can be contended that such policies must be more ambitious if they are to do enough to narrow the gap between rich and poor and thus engender the solidarity required for the Union to deal properly with the problems that confront it, particularly when Central and East European countries accede. The Union is also relevant to the relationship between enterprises and employees in the member-states, since the breaking down of frontiers within the single market removes from them some of the instruments with which they have sought to balance that relationship. The intention of the Maastricht Treaty's Social Chapter has been to enable the Union to restore some of these instruments at the European level.

Second, the idea of democratic autonomy can be seen as relevant to the Union by those who believe that the solidarity necessary for it to sustain a democratic structure needs to be based on a common conception of democracy which goes beyond the classical model. Held has argued that, because the problems which face modern societies require not only democratic autonomy but also democracy beyond the nation-state, national democracies require a form of 'international cosmopolitan democracy' that caters for both, if they are to be 'sustained and developed in the contemporary era'.[31]

Whether democratic autonomy is regarded as a necessary complement to liberal democracy or not, the prospective enlargement to a dozen or more countries of Central and Eastern Europe presents a new problem for the European Union. The majority of states that have joined the founder member-states so far have been well established democracies: Britain, Ireland, Denmark, Finland, Sweden and Austria. The countries with recent experience of dictatorship were few and not at all likely to relapse. The prospects for some of the Central and East European countries may be more doubtful; and there are more of them. The Union has policies to help consolidate democracy in those states.[32] This is in the Union's interests because democracies make better neighbours; and the prospect of their accession adds a sharp edge to that motive, since member-states which depart from democracy would present a very severe problem to the Union.

Much attention has been paid to the question of how best to help establish effective market economies in those countries. Help in the establishment of working democracies is no less important.

While states from other continents will not be valid candidates for accession to the Union, Europeans have an interest in the establishment of new democracies there as well, and in the consolidation of existing ones. The market economies that accompany pluralist democracy make better trading partners; and relations between well established democracies are more peaceful and secure.[33] Such democracies could also participate in the development of transnational institutions with pre-democratic elements in the wider world. But meanwhile, it is the Europeans who have to decide whether to adopt such structures by reforming the institutions of the European Union.

The British and European democracy

The relationship between Britain and the European Community, now the Union, during the first quarter-century of British membership has not been a happy one. Among the reasons for this, one may be insufficient understanding of the history of Britain's relations with the continent. This book has shown how much the British polity gained from elements of democracy that had been developed in the Low Countries and how much the Americans and subsequently other Europeans in turn gained from the British, accepting the principles of representative government and the rule of law based on rights. The extent to which all the states of Western Europe, and increasingly those of Central and Eastern Europe, have based their constitutions and their political practice on these principles, which the British therefore now share with them, is not always appreciated in Britain.

The stages in development of democracy depicted in the preceding chapters also show how modern democracy evolved through stages of pre-democratic institutions. Seen in this perspective, the present institutions of the European Union, poised between inter-governmental diplomacy and federal democracy, may be more comprehensible. The British may decide that they wish to take part in developing European democracy or they may wish to stand aside. It is to be hoped that the decision will be based on awareness not only of the problems involved in establishing a European democracy, but also of the potential for such democracy and the contribution that the British themselves can make to it.

Notes

Chapter 1: The Development of European Democracy

1. Robert A. Dahl, *Democracy and its Critics* (New Haven, CT: Yale University Press, 1989), p.316.
2. Ibid., pp.2, 18–20, 317–18.
3. See, for example, David Held, *Models of Democracy* (Cambridge: Polity Press, 1989), pp.254–64.
4. See Laski's letter of 2 November 1919 to Russell, in Bertrand Russell, *The Autobiography of Bertrand Russell, 1914–1944* (London: George Allen and Unwin, 1968), p.113.
5. Dahl, *Democracy*, pp.2, 318–20.
6. David Held, *Democracy and the Global Order: From the Modern State to Cosmopolitan Governance* (Cambridge: Polity Press, 1995), pp.32, 73, 143, 227.

Chapter 2: Mediaeval Flanders and the Seeds of Modern Democracy

1. There are two modern editions of Galbert's Latin narrative: H. Pirenne (ed.), *Histoire du meurtre de Charles le Bon, comte de Flandre (1127–1128) par Galbert de Bruges* (Paris: Picard, 1891) and J. Rider, *Galbertus Notarius Brugensis. De multro, traditione, et occisione gloriosi Karoli comitis Flandriarum* (Turnhout: Brepols, 1994, Corpus Christianorum. Continuatio Mediaeualis, LXXXI). Dutch, English and French translations also exist (with extensive introductions): *Galbert of Bruges, the Murder of Charles the Good*, trans. J.B. Ross (Toronto: Toronto University Press, 1984, Medieval Academy Reprints for Teaching); R.C. Van Caenegem (ed.), *Galbert van Brugge, grafelijk secretaris: De moord op Karel de Goede: Dagboek van de gebeurtenissen in de jaren 1127–1128*, trans. A. Demyttenaere (Antwerp: Mercatorfonds, 1978), and R.C. Van Caenegem (ed.), *Galbert de Bruges, secrétaire comtal: Le meurtre de Charles le Bon*, trans. J. Gengoux (Antwerp: Fonds Mercator, 1978).
2. See C.H. Haskins, *The Renaissance of the Twelfth Century* (Cambridge, MA: Harvard University Press, 1927) and C.N.L. Brooke, *The Twelfth Century Renaissance* (London/New York: Thames and Hudson, 1969).
3. See R.C. Van Caenegem, 'Galbert of Bruges on Serfdom, Prosecution of Crime and Constitutionalism', in B.S. Bachrach and D. Nicholas (eds), *Law, Custom, and the Social Fabric in Medieval Europe: Essays in Honor of Bryce Lyon* (Kalamazoo: Western Michigan University Press, 1990), pp.89–112.
4. For the Flemish keuren in general, see F.L. Ganshof, 'La Flandre', in F. Lot and R. Fawtier (eds), *Histoire des institutions françaises au moyen âge. I: Institutions seigneuriales* (Paris: PUF, 1957), pp.343–426. For the oldest extensive Flemish borough charter, see R.C. Van Caenegem, 'The Borough Charter of Saint-Omer of 1127, Granted by William Clito, Count of Flanders', in R.C. Van Caenegem, *Legal History: A European Perspective* (London and Rio Grande: Hambledon Press, 1991), pp.61–70.

5. R.C. Van Caenegem, *Geschiedenis van het strafrecht in Vlaanderen van de XIe tot de XIVe eeuw* (Brussels: Koninklijke Vlaamse Academie voor Wetenschappen, Letteren en Schone Kunsten van België, 1954, Verhandlingen Kon. Acad. Wetensch., Klasse der Letteren, no. 19), pp.14–17.

6. R.C. Van Caenegem, *An Historical Introduction to Western Constitutional Law* (Cambridge: Cambridge University Press, 1995), pp.15–21.

7. Pirenne, *Histoire du meurtre de Charles le Bon*, pp.138–41. See the comments by Van Caenegem in *Galbert of Bruges*, pp.102–7 and R.C. Van Caenegem, 'The Ghent Revolt of February 1128', in L. Milis et al. (eds), R.C. Van Caenegem, *Law, History, the Low Countries and Europe* (London and Rio Grande: Hambledon Press, 1994), pp.107–12.

8. Pirenne, *Histoire du meurtre de Charles le Bon*, cc.93, 94 and 95, pp.137–41.

9. V. Fris, *Histoire de Gand depuis les origines jusqu'en 1913* (Ghent: Tavernier, 1930), pp.126–7.

10. For recent surveys, see D. Waley, *The Italian City-Republics* (London: Longman, 1978), and J.H. Mundy, 'In Praise of Italy: the Italian Republics', *Speculum* 64, 1989, pp.815–34.

11. P. Carson, *James Van Artevelde: The Man from Ghent* (Ghent: Story-Scientia, 1980).

12. See J. Decavele (ed.), *Ghent: In Defence of a Rebellious City: History, Art, Culture* (Antwerp: Mercatorfonds, 1989). For the position of Ghent in the earlier phase of the Burgundian state, see M. Boone, *Gent en de Bourgondische hertogen ca. 1384–ca. 1453: een sociaal-politieke studie van een staatsvorm-ingsproces* (Brussels: Paleis van der Academiën, 1990, Verhand. Kon. Acad. Wetensch., Kl. Lett., Jg. 52, no. 133).

13. The most recent discussion of the republican strain, which started in the mediaeval cities of Flanders and culminated in the independent Dutch Republic, can be found in W. Blockmans, 'De tweekoppige draak. Het Gentse stadsbestuur tussen vorst en onderdanen, 14e–16e eeuw', in J. de Zutter, L. Charles and A. Capiteyn (eds), *Qui valet ingenio: Liber Amicorum J. Decavele* (Ghent: Stichting Mens en Kultur, 1996), pp.27–37. The author stresses the leading role of Ghent and analyses several plans of Ghent, Bruges and Ypres for the division of the county of Flanders into three city-states, with a common monarch who would, however, depend on the recognition of his subjects and only wield limited power. The author underlines the fact that, two years before the Act of Abjuration, the city of Ghent had, on 6 August 1579, already renounced Philip II as legitimate ruler: the king was said to have rejected reasonable proposals of peace so that his sovereignty had passed to the urban magistrate.

14. Blockmans, 'De tweekoppige draak', p.34. The author (p.32) shows the pre-ponderance of Flanders and Brabant by referring to the contribution of those two principalities in the total tax yield of the Netherlands. Indeed, the distribution of the taxation, established by the Estates General at the time of Emperor Charles V, was as follows: Flanders paid 34 per cent, Brabant 29 per cent, Holland and Zeeland together between 15 and 17 per cent, Guelderland 12 per cent, and the other regions much less.

15. See J. Gilissen, *Le régime représentatif avant 1790 en Belgique* (Brussels: La Renaissance du Livre, 1952), and C. Van De Kieft, 'De Staten-Generaal in het Bourgondisch-Oostenrijkse Tijdvak (1464–1555)', in S.J. Fockema Andreae

(ed.), *500 Jaren Staten-Generaal in de Nederlanden* (Assen: Van Gorcum, 1964), pp.1–26.

16. I am thinking of W. Prevenier, A. Zoete and W.P. Blockmans, editors of the *Handelingen van de Leden en Staten van Vlaanderen* for the Belgian Royal Commission for History since 1959.

17. It is of some importance to realise how the members of the Third Estate – that is, the burgesses (comparable to some extent to the English House of Commons) – were appointed, both in the earlier stage of the 'aldermen of Flanders' (scabini Flandriae) and later. Generally speaking, the aldermen of the Flemish boroughs were, in the twelfth century, appointed by the count and, in the thirteenth, coopted by the sitting aldermen; whereas the fourteenth century witnessed a democratisation by which the common people, organised in guilds, crafts and corporations, played a dominant role in the selection of the town authorities and their spokesmen who sat in the urban 'general assemblies'. Nowhere in mediaeval Europe do we find the modern-type democracy with general franchise and secret ballot. Nevertheless, the numerous assemblies and estates of the later Middle Ages show that they could, in the course of time, develop into representative bodies as we know them in the modern democracies.

18. Everything was ready, in 1473, for Charles the Bold to be made king of Lotharingia (a name going back to Carolingian times) by Emperor Frederick III who, however, withdrew at the last moment. So the Burgundian Netherlands remained what they had been before: that is, a union of principalities held together by a common ruler (who was count of Flanders, Hainaut, Holland and Namur, Duke of Brabant, etc.) and by ever-expanding common institutions. The title of king, which eluded the Burgundian dukes, would have been a consummation of what was in fact their status as princes with most of the attributes of kings.

19. See the recent survey by W. Prevenier and W. Blockmans, *De Bourgondische Nederlanden* (Antwerp: Mercatorfonds, 1983).

20. Ibid., p.198.

21. Ibid.

22. R.C. Van Caenegem, 'Methods of Proof in Western Medieval Law', in Van Caenegem, *Legal History*, pp.71–113; R. Bartlett, *Trial by Fire and Water: The Medieval Judicial Ordeal* (Oxford: Clarendon Press, 1986); R.C. Van Caenegem, 'Reflexions on rational and irrational modes of proof in medieval Europe', *The Legal History Review* 58, 1990, pp.263–79.

23. Van Caenegem, *Geschiedenis*, pp.280–307.

24. Pirenne, *Histoire du meurtre de Charles le Bon*, c.55, p.87. See the comments in R.C. Van Caenegem, 'Considerations on the customary law of twelfth-century Flanders', in Van Caenegem, *Law, History, the Low Countries and Europe*, pp.97–106. In the following centuries the towns produced a considerable body of legislation. For some recent surveys, see J.-M. Cauchies, 'Services publics et législation dans les villes des anciens Pays-Bas: Questions d'heuristique et de méthode', in *L'initiative publique des communes en Belgique: Fondements historiques*. Actes du 11e Coll. internat. Crédit communal de Belgique (1–4 September 1982) (Brussels, 1984), pp.639–88; P.Godding, 'Les ordonnances des autorités urbaines au moyen âge: Leur apport à la technique législative', in J.-M. Duvosquel and E. Thoen (eds), *Peasants and townsmen in medieval*

Europe: Studia in honorem A. Verhulst (Ghent: Snoek Ducaju, 1995), pp.185–201.

25. F. Vercauteren (ed.), *Actes des Comtes de Flandre, 1071–1128* (Brussels: Palais des Académies, 1938, Commission Royale d'Histoire), 79, p.178.

26. Pirenne, *Histoire du meurtre de Charles le Bon*, cc.105, 108, pp.150, 154–5.

27. R.C. Van Caenegem and L. Milis, 'Kritische uitgave van de "Grote Keure" van Filips van de Elzas, graaf van Vlaanderen, voor Gent en Brugge (1165–1177)', *Handelingen van de Koninklijke Commissie voor Geschiedenis* 143, 1977, pp.207–57.

28. Pirenne, *Histoire du meurtre de Charles le Bon*, c.106, p.152.

29. F.L. Ganshof, 'Les origines du concept de souveraineté nationale en Flandre', *Revue d'Histoire du Droit* 18, 1950, pp.135–58.

30. See J. Van der Grinten, 'Het Plakkaat van Verlatinge', in *Bijdragen Vaderl. Geschiedenis en Oudheidkunde*, 5th series, II, 1932, pp.161–78; J.P.A. Coopmans, 'Het Plakkaat van Verlatinge (1581) en de Declaration of Independence (1776)', in *Bijdragen en Mededelingen Geschied. Nederlanden* 98, 1983, pp.540–67.

31. See S.J. Fockema Andreae, *De Nederlandse Staat onder de Republiek* (Amsterdam: Noord-Hollandse Uitgevermaatschappij, 1961, 3rd edition, 1969), pp.3–5.

32. See the classic survey in Ganshof, 'La Flandre', and the recent detailed monograph by S. Dauchy, *De processen in beroep uit Vlaanderen bij het Parlement van Parijs (1320–1521). Een rechtshistorisch onderzoek naar de wording van staat en souvereiniteit in de Bourgondisch-Habsburgse periode* (Brussels: Paleis der Academiën, 1995, Verhand. Kon. Acad. Wetensch., Kl. Lett., Jg. 37, no. 154).

33. See F.L. Ganshof, *Vlaanderen onder de eerste graven* (Antwerp: Standaard, 1944).

34. F.L. Ganshof, 'Trois mandements perdus du roi de France Louis VI intéressant la Flandre', in *Handelingen Genootschap Emulation de Bruges*, 87, 1950, pp.115–33; F.L. Ganshof, 'Le roi de France en Flandre en 1127 et 1128', *Revue historique de droit français et étranger*, 4th series, 27, 1949, pp.204–28.

35. See F. Dickmann, *Der Westfälische Frieden* (Münster: Aschendorff, 1965).

36. R.C. Van Caenegem, *An Historical Introduction to Western Constitutional Law*, pp.142–50.

37. H. Pirenne, *Les anciennes démocraties des Pays-Bas* (Paris: Flammarion, 1910) was published in English as *Belgian Democracy: Its Early History* (Manchester, 1915) and in paperback as *Early Democracies in the Low Countries: Urban Society and Political Conflict in the Middle Ages and the Renaissance* (New York: Harper and Row, 1963). See, on Pirenne, B. Lyon, *Henri Pirenne: A biographical and intellectual study* (Ghent: Story-Scientia, 1974); R.C. Van Caenegem, 'Henri Pirenne: Medievalist and Historian of Belgium', in Van Caenegem, *Law, History, the Low Countries and Europe*, pp.161–78.

38. D. Lambrecht (ed.), *Acta Processus circa Synodum: Proces gevoerd door Brugge, Damme en het Vrije tegen de bisschop van Doornik voor de officialiteit te Reims en de Curie te Rome 1269–ca. 1301* (Brussels: Ministerie van Justitie, 1988, Kon. Com. Oude Wetten. Verzameling van de Oude Rechtspraak in België, 7th series).

39. Text in J. Van Der Straeten, *Het charter en de raad van Kortenberg*, II (Leuven: University of Leuven, Brussels, 1952), no. 1, pp.12–14, and in H.P.H. Camps, *Oorkondenboek van Noord Brabant*, I (The Hague: Nijhoff, 1979), Rijks Geschiedkundige Publicatiën 883, pp.1074ff. See the comparative-historical comments in B. Lyon, 'Fact and Fiction in English and Belgian Constitutional Law', *Medievalia et Humanistica*, 10, 1956, pp.82–101.

40. See, for a survey in English by a famous historian, P.C.A. Geyl, *The Revolt of the Netherlands 1555–1601* (London: Williams and Norgate, 1932); see also Chapter 3, this volume, by E.H. Kossmann. For the rise of protestantism in Flanders see J. Decavele, *De dageraad van de Reformatie in Vlaanderen (1520–1565)*, 2 vols (Brussels: Paleis der Academiën, 1975, Verhand. Kon. Acad. Wetensch., Kl. Lett., Jg. 37, no. 76). The reader will find an interesting collection of texts (1570–87) in M. Van Gelderen (ed.), *The Dutch Revolt* (Cambridge: Cambridge University Press, 1993, Cambridge Texts in the History of Political Thought).

41. C. Brinton, *The Anatomy of Revolution* (New York: Random House, 1965).

42. See, for a general but brief survey, R.C. Van Caenegem, 'Reflexions on the Place of the Low Countries in European Legal History', in Van Caenegem, *Legal History*, pp.149–63.

43. When we say that in the Burgundian Netherlands the state came before the nation, the reader may wonder why we, following Ganshof, already speak of 'national sovereignty' at the time of Galbert of Bruges; but it should be realised that a national feeling in the respective principalities, such as Flanders, Brabant and Holland, had existed for centuries before those provinces were lifted, in Burgundian times, into a wider pan-Netherlandish statehood and a new, wider political identity.

44. H.G. Richardson and G.O. Sayles, *Parliaments and Great Councils in Medieval England* (London: Stevens, 1961); E.B. Fryde and E. Miller (eds), *Historical Studies of the English Parliament*, 2 vols (Cambridge: Cambridge University Press, 1970); G.O. Sayles, *The Functions of the Medieval Parliament of England* (London and Ronceverte: Hambledon Press, 1988).

45. D. Lambrecht and J. Van Rompaey, 'De staatsinstellingen in het Zuiden van de 11de tot de 14de eeuw', in *Algemene Geschiedenis der Nederlanden*, III, Haarlem, 1982, pp.129–34.

46. For Thierry, see *Nationaal Biografisch Woordenboek*, XIII (Brussels: Paleis der Acadamiën, 1990), cols 224–42 (by Th. De Hemptinne). For Philip, see ibid., IV, 1970, cols 290–329 (by H. Van Werveke). For Baldwin IX, see ibid., I, 1964, cols 224–37 (by W. Prevenier).

47. See R.C. Van Caenegem, 'Reflections on the History of England', in Van Caenegem, *Law, History, the Low Countries and Europe*, pp.37–54.

Chapter 3: Republican Freedom against Monarchical Absolutism: The Dutch Experience in the Seventeenth Century

1. Staatsregeling voor het Bataafsche volk (1 mei 1798): 'Het Bataafsche volk, zig vornemende tot eenen ondeelbaaren Staat . . .'.

2. L. de Gou (ed.), *Het ontwerp van Constitutie van 1797*, vol. 1, pp.173–4 (The Hague: Rijks Geschiedkundige Publicatiën, Kleine Serie 55, 1983).

3. For a synopsis of the problem, see H. Daalder, 'Oud-republikeinse veelheid en democratisering in Nederland' (1987), reprinted in H. Daalder, B.A.G.M. Tromp and J. Th. J. van den Berg, *Politiek en Historie: opstellen over Nederlandse politiek en vergelijkende politieke wetenschap* (Amsterdam: Bakker, 1990), pp.64–80.
4. Printed in English translation in E.H. Kossmann and A.F. Mellink, *Texts Concerning the Revolt of the Netherlands* (Cambridge: Cambridge University Press, 1974), pp.165–77.
5. Ibid., pp.216–28.
6. R. Fruin and H.T. Colenbrander, *Geschiedenis van de staatsinstellingen in Nederland tot den val der Republiek* (The Hague: Nijhoff, 1901, 2nd edition, 1922, reprinted by Martinus Nijhoff with an important introduction by I. Schöffer, 1980) is still the best compendium, though S.J. Fockema Andreae, *De Nederlandse staat onder de Republiek* (Amsterdam: Noord-Hollandse Uitgevermaatschappij, 1961, 3rd edition, 1969) has distinct merits. Jonathan I. Israel's recent *The Dutch Republic: Its Rise, Greatness and Fall, 1477–1806* (Oxford: Clarendon Press, 1995, pb 1999) gives lucid surveys of the institutions and offers original interpretations of their working.
7. Cf. I. Schöffer's lively inaugural lecture, *Ons tweede tijdvak* (Leiden, 1962), reprinted in his *Veelvormig verleden* (Amsterdam: De Bataafsche Leeuw, 1987), pp.15–25.
8. See the detailed analysis by the Canadian historian F.G. Oosterhof, *Leicester and the Netherlands 1586–1587* (Utrecht: HES Publishers, 1988).
9. Kossmann and Mellink, *Texts*, pp.272–3.
10. Ibid., *Texts*, pp.274–81.

Chapter 4: William III, the Glorious Revolution and the Development of Parliamentary Democracy in Britain

1. See Mark Goldie, 'The Revolution of 1689 and the Structure of Political Argument', *Bulletin of Research in the Humanities* 83 (1980), pp.473–564; Richard Ashcraft, *Revolutionary Politics and Locke's Two Treatises of Government* (Princeton, NJ/Guildford: Princeton University Press, 1986), pp.39–74, 600.
2. See the excellent recent essay by W.A. Speck, 'Britain and the Dutch Republic', in K. Davids and J. Lucassen (eds), *A Miracle Mirrored: The Dutch Republic in European Perspective* (Cambridge: Cambridge University Press, 1995), pp.173–83.
3. Ibid., p.176.
4. Ashcraft, *Revolutionary Politics*, pp.591–600.
5. J.I. Israel, 'The Dutch Role in the Glorious Revolution', in Jonathan I. Israel (ed.), *The Anglo-Dutch Moment. Essays on the Glorious Revolution and its World Impact* (Cambridge: Cambridge University Press, 1991), pp.138–60.
6. In fact, 'one school' here is something of a misnomer as the tendency to deny that anything significant happened in 1688–89, which has long been the view of marxist historians such as Christopher Hill, is also the view of some particularly right-wing revisionists such as Jonathan Clark: see the discussion of 1688 in J.C.D. Clark, *English Society, 1688–1832* (Cambridge: Cambridge

University Press, 1985); see also W.A. Speck, 'Some Consequences of the Glorious Revolution', in D. Hoak and M. Feingold (eds), *The World of William and Mary* (Stanford, CA: Stanford University Press, 1996), pp.29–32.

7. 'Whatever modifications we may make to the classical Whig interpretation', observes Hugh Trevor-Roper, 'in the end it is difficult to contest Macaulay's thesis, that the English Revolution of 1688 saved England from a different kind of revolution a century later.' See H.R. Trevor-Roper, 'The Glorious Revolution of 1688', in H.R. Trevor-Roper, *From Counter-Reformation to Glorious Revolution* (London: Secker and Warburg, 1992), p.247.

8. Israel, 'The Dutch Role', pp.123–46; Robert Beddard, *A Kingdom without a King. The Journal of the Provisional Government in the Revolution of 1688* (Oxford: Phaidon, 1988), pp.17–31; Tony Claydon, *William III and the Godly Revolution* (Cambridge: Cambridge University Press, 1996), pp.122–4. On the weakness of James's field army on Salisbury Plain and estimate of its size at about 12,000 men, see BJ MS Add. 34510, 'Van Citters to States General', London, 7 December 1688.

9. Israel, 'The Dutch Role', pp.126–31; J.I. Israel, 'William III and Toleration', in O.P. Grell, J.I. Israel and N. Tyacke (eds), *From Persecution to Toleration: The Glorious Revolution and Religion in England* (Oxford: Clarendon Press, 1991), pp.146–9.

10. See Claydon, *William III and the Godly Revolution*, pp.26–8, 228–36; see also Tony Claydon, 'William III's *Declaration of Reasons* and the Glorious Revolution', *The Historical Journal* 39 (1996), pp.87–108.

11. On the orchestration of William III's propaganda campaign in the autumn of 1688, see Jonathan I. Israel, 'Propaganda in the Making of the Glorious Revolution', in Susan Roach (ed.), *Across the Narrow Seas: Studies in the History and Bibliography of Britain and the Low Countries presented to Anna E.C. Simoni* (London: British Library, 1991), pp.167–77; Israel, 'The Dutch Role', pp.121–4.

12. Edmund Bohun, *The History of the Desertion* (London: 1689), p.123.

13. *His Majesties Gracious Letter to the Meeting of the Estates of His Ancient Kingdom of Scotland* (dated 17 May 1689), (Edinburgh: 1689), p.1.

14. *His Majesties Most Gracious Speech to both Houses of Parliament, on Friday the Fourth Day of November 1692* (London: 1692), p.4.

15. *The Declaration of the Lords and Commons Assembled at Westminster, presented to their Highnesses the Prince and Princess of Orange, at Whitehall the 13th of February, 1688/9*, p.2; see also Lois Schwoerer, 'Propaganda in the Revolution of 1688–9', *American Historical Review* 82 (1977), pp.843–74.

16. For a reminder that Parliament and the people were 'incouraged to the demand of their Rights by the Declaration of his Highness the Prince of Orange', see *A Letter to Doctor Lancaster, Wherein The Resistance of the People Under the Conduct of the Prince of Orange And the Placing of King William on the Throne Are Vindicated from the Odious Imputation of Usurpation and Rebellion* (London: 1697), p.7.

17. Israel, 'The Dutch Role', pp.160–2.

18. For comparisons between the armada of 1588 and that of 1688, see Jonathan I. Israel and Geoffrey Parker, 'Of Providence and Protestant Winds: the Spanish Armada of 1588 and the Dutch Armada of 1688', in Israel, *The Anglo-Dutch Moment*, pp.335–64.

19. Israel, 'The Dutch Role', pp.117–20.
20. K.H.D. Haley, *The British and the Dutch* (London: George Philip, 1988), pp.136–41; J.L. Price, 'William III, England and the Balance of Power in Europe', *Groniek. Gronings Historisch Tijdschrift* 101 (1988), pp.68–9.

Chapter 5: The United States Constitution and its Roots in British Political Thought and Tradition

1. Michael Kraus, *The Atlantic Civilization: Eighteenth-Century Origins* (Ithaca, NY: Cornell University Press, 1949), p.26.
2. Edmund Burke, quoted in H.T. Dickinson, 'The Eighteenth-Century Debate on the Sovereignty of Parliament', *Transactions of the Royal Historical Society*, 5th series, 25 (1976), p.199.
3. Gareth Jones (ed.), *The Sovereignty of the Law: Selections from Blackstone's Commentaries on the Laws of England* (London: Macmillan, 1973), pp.71–2; J.G.A. Pocock, *Politics, Language and Time* (London: Methuen, 1972), p.132.
4. Gordon S. Wood, *The Creation of the American Republic, 1776–1787* (Chapel Hill, NC: University of North Carolina Press, 1969), pp.49–50.
5. J.G.A. Pocock, *The Machiavellian Moment* (Princeton, NJ: Princeton University Press, 1975), esp. pp.506–52.
6. David L. Jacobson (ed.), *The English Libertarian Heritage* (Indianapolis: Bobbs-Merrill, 1965), pp.106, 131, 91, 93; David N. Mayer, 'The English Radical Whig Origins of American Constitutionalism', *Washington University Law Quarterly* 70 (1991), pp.131–207.
7. James Burgh, *Political Disquisitions* (3 vols) (London: 1774–75), III, pp.277–8; I, pp.3–4.
8. Colin Bonwick, *English Radicals and the American Revolution* (Chapel Hill, NC: University of North Carolina Press, 1977), pp.17–26.
9. Thomas R. Adams, *American Independence: The Growth of an Idea* (Providence, RI: Brown University Press, 1965); H. Trevor Colbourn, *The Lamp of Experience: Whig History and the Intellectual Origins of the American Revolution* (Chapel Hill, NC: University of North Carolina Press, 1965).
10. John Dickinson, 'August 13, 1787', in Max Farrand (ed.), *The Records of the Federal Convention of 1787* (revised edition in 4 vols) (New Haven, CT:Yale University Press, 1937), II, p.278.
11. Richard Bland, in Merrill Jensen (ed.), *Tracts of the American Revolution: 1763–1776* (Indianapolis: Bobbs-Merrill, 1967), p.125.
12. William Riker, 'Dutch and American Federalism', *Journal of the History of Ideas* 18 (1957), pp.495–521; Robert A. Rutland et al. (eds), *The Papers of James Madison*, vols IV and X (Chicago, IL: University of Chicago Press, 1975, 1977): IX, pp.11–18; X, pp.81, 82–3n, 88, 89n, 101, 189, 210, 274, 320–4, 364, 406.
13. Winton U. Solberg (ed.), *The Federal Convention and the Formation of the Union of the American States* (New York: The Liberal Arts Press, 1958), p.9; S.E. Morison (ed.), *Sources and Documents Illustrating the American Revolution, 1764–1788 and the Formation of the Federal Constitution* (2nd edition; Oxford: Clarendon Press, 1929), p.33.

14. Alfred H. Kelly et al., *The American Constitution: Its Origins and Development* (6th edition; New York: W.W. Norton, 1983), p.27.
15. Dumas Malone, *Jefferson and His Time* (6 vols) (Boston: Little, Brown, 1948–81), pp.70–2.
16. Bernard Bailyn, *The Ideological Origins of the American Revolution* (Cambridge, MA: The Belknap Press of Harvard University Press, 1967), pp.55–6.
17. James Madison in Marvin Meyers (ed.), *The Mind of the Founder* (Indianapolis: Bobbs-Merrill, 1973), p.512; John Adams in Lester J. Cappon (ed.), *The Complete Correspondence Between Thomas Jefferson and John Adams* (2 vols) (Chapel Hill, NC: University of North Carolina Press, 1959), II, p.463.
18. William Hooper in Elisha P. Douglass, *Rebels and Democrats* (Chicago, IL: Quadrangle Books, 1965 [1955]), p.123.
19. Jack P. Greene, *Peripheries and Center: Constitutional Development in the Extended Polities of the British Empire and the United States, 1607–1788* (Athens, GA: University of Georgia Press, 1986), p.173; quotation from Peter Onuf, *Origins of the Federal Republic: Jurisdictional Controversies in the United States, 1775–1787* (Philadelphia, PA: University of Pennsylvania Press, 1983), pp.21–2.
20. Wood, *The Creation*, pp.260–1.
21. Mayer, 'English Radical Whig Origins', p.144.
22. Morison (ed.), *Sources and Documents*, p.149.
23. The Bill of Rights, 1689, 1 Will. & Mar. Sess. 2, c.2.; US Constitution and Amendments I to X.
24. K.M. Stampp, 'The Concept of a Perpetual Union', *Journal of American History* 65 (1978), p.11.
25. Forrest McDonald, *Novus Ordo Seclorum: The Intellectual Origins of the Constitution* (Lawrence, KS: University Press of Kansas, 1985), p.209.
26. Greene, *Peripheries*, p.213.
27. Theodore Lowi, *The Personal President* (Ithaca, NY: Cornell University Press, 1985), p.24.
28. Walter Bagehot, *The English Constitution*, ed. R.H.S. Crossman (London: Collins, 1963), p.94.
29. Daniel J. Boorstin, *The Mysterious Science of the Law* (Gloucester, MA: Peter Smith, 1973 [1941]), pp.3–4.
30. J.R.T. Hughes, *Social Control in the Colonial Economy* (Charlottesville, VA: University Press of Virginia, 1976), p.86.
31. Colin Bonwick, 'The Regulation of Political Power', in R.A. Burchell (ed.), *The End of Anglo-America* (Manchester: Manchester University Press, 1991), pp.1–23.

Chapter 6: Proudhon and Anti-jacobin Federalism

1. See, in particular, Daniel Mornet, *Les Origines intellectuelles de la Révolution française* (Paris: Colin, 2nd edition, 1934), part 3, ch. viii; A. Aulard, *Histoire politique de la Révolution française* (Paris: Colin, 3rd edition, 1905), pp.19ff.
2. *Le Moniteur*, vol. XVII, p.252.
3. J.-J. Rousseau, *Du Contrat social*, II–IV.

4. P.-J. Proudhon, Letter of 17 May 1845, *Correspondance: édition Langlois* (Paris: Librairie internationale A. Lacroix, 1874–75).
5. P.-J. Proudhon, *Premier mémoire sur la propriété*, 1840 (reprinted Paris: Librairie Marcel Rivière, 1926), p.346.
6. P.-J. Proudhon, *De l'utilité de la célébration du Dimanche*, 1839 (reprinted Paris: Rivière, 1926), p.61.
7. P.-J. Proudhon, *Système des Contradictions économiques ou Philosophie de la Misère*, 1846 (reprinted Paris: Rivière, 1923). Marx's ironic and unfair riposte, *The Poverty of Philosophy*, was published in the following year.
8. P.-J. Proudhon, *Idée générale de la Révolution au XIXe siècle,* 1849 (reprinted Paris: Rivière, 1923), p.395.
9. See Max Stirner, *Der Einzige und sein Eigentum* (Berlin: 1845).
10. Proudhon, *Premier mémoire*, p.131.
11. P.-J. Proudhon, *De la Justice dans la Révolution et dans l'Église*, 1858, much enlarged 2nd edition, 1860 (reprinted Paris: Rivière, 1930), and P.-J. Proudhon, *Corpus des oeuvres de philosophie en langue française* (Paris: Fayard, 1988).
12. P.-J. Proudhon, *Les confessions d'un Révolutionnaire*, 1849 (reprinted Paris: Rivière, 1920).
13. Proudhon, *Idée générale de la Révolution.*
14. Proudhon, *De la Justice.*
15. Proudhon, *Premier mémoire*, p.144.
16. P.-J. Proudhon, *La Guerre et la Paix,* 1861 (reprinted Paris: Rivière, 1927).
17. Proudhon, *Correspondance*, X, pp.38–9, 1860.
18. P.-J. Proudhon, *Du Principe fédératif et de la nécessité de reconstituer le Parti de la Révolution*, 1863 (reprinted Paris: Rivière, 1959).
19. P.-J. Proudhon, *De la Capacité politique des classes ouvrières*, 1865, posthumous (reprinted Paris: Rivière, 1924).
20. Proudhon, *Du Principe fédératif*, p.319.

Chapter 7: Anglo-saxon Influences and the Development of German Democracy after World War Two

1. Walter Vogel and Christoph Weisz (eds), *Akten zur Vorgeschichte der Bundesrepublik Deutschland 1945–1949*, vol. 1, Hrsg Bundesarchiv und Institut für Zeitgeschichte (München/Wien: R. Oldenbourg, 1976), pp.125–6.
2. Ibid., pp.151ff.
3. See Anthony Glees, 'The British and the Germans, 1945–92, From Enemies to Partners', in Christian Soe and Dirk Verheyen (eds), *The Germans and their Neighbors* (Colorado: Westview Press, 1993, pb 1995).
4. Noel Annan, *Changing Enemies: The Defeat and Regeneration of Germany* (London: HarperCollins, 1995), p.211.
5. See Anthony Glees, *Re-inventing Germany: German Political Development since 1945* (Oxford: Berg, 1996).
6. See Dick de Mildt, *In the Name of the People: Perpetrators of Genocide in the Reflection of their Post-War Prosecution in West Germany* (The Hague: Martinus Nijhoff, 1996). Some recent German research concludes, moreover, that West Germany's successful overcoming of Nazism probably owed more to the determination of Germany's western occupiers than to the Germans

themselves and singles out British action against old and new Nazis as an important case in point. Following the initial process of de-Nazification, the Allies' latent threat to intervene if necessary had an effect on the development of the Federal Republic that can hardly be exaggerated; see Norbert Frei, *Vergangenheitspolitik: Die Anfänge der Bundesrepublik und die NS-Vergangenheit*, 2, durchgesehene Auflage (München: C.H. Beck, 1997), pp.368–72, 376–84, 400. See also Anthony Glees, 'The Making of British Policy on War Crimes: History as Politics in Great Britain', *Contemporary European History*, vol. 1, no. 2, 1992, pp.171–97, and 'War Crimes: the Security and Intelligence Policy Dimension', *Intelligence and National Security*, vol. 7, no. 3, July 1992, pp.242–67.

7. Quoted in Robin Day, *But with Respect: Memorable Interviews with Statesmen and Parliamentarians* (London: Weidenfeld and Nicolson, 1993), pp.123ff.
8. Wolfgang Krieger, *General Lucius D. Clay und die amerikanische Deutschlandpolitik 1945–1949* (Stuttgart: Klett-Cotta, 1987), p.11. See also Jeffry M. Diefendorf, Axel Frohn and Hermann-Josef Rupieper (eds), *American Policy and the Reconstruction of West Germany, 1945–1955* (Cambridge: Cambridge University Press, 1993); Ralph Willett, *The Americanization of Germany* (London: Routledge, 1989); Hans Wallenberg, *Report on Democratic Institutions in Germany* (Westport, CT: Greenwood Press, 1956); Edward N. Peterson, *The American Occupation of Germany* (Detroit, MI: Wayne State University Press, 1978).
9. Interview with Robert Lochner, Berlin 6 December 1995.
10. See Vogel and Weisz, *Akten zur Vorgeschichte.*
11. Ibid., pp.32, 59. The authors suggest the British were always 'more careful and distant' in their dealings with German political leaders.
12. See Roger Morgan, *The United States and West Germany 1945–73: a study in alliance politics* (London: Oxford University Press, 1974), pp.16–17.
13. See Krieger, *General Lucius D. Clay*, esp. pp.310ff.
14. Ivone Kirkpatrick, *The Inner Circle: Memoirs of Ivone Kirkpatrick* (London: Macmillan, 1959), p.205. See also Anthony Glees, *Exile Politics During the Second World War* (Oxford: Oxford University Press, 1982), pp.142–3. Interview with Sir Frank Roberts, 28 June 1979.
15. Annan, *Changing Enemies*, p.157.
16. Ibid., pp.184, 185, 215.
17. Curt Garner, 'Public Service Personnel in West Germany in the 1950s', *The Journal of Social History* 29, 1995/96, pp.25–80.
18. See Michael Balfour, *West Germany* (London: Benn, 1968), pp.188–90.
19. For the drafting of the Basic Law, see Kurt Sontheimer, *The Government and Politics of West Germany* (London: Hutchinson, 1972), pp.29–32; Alfred Grosser, *Germany in our Time* (Harmondsworth: Penguin, 1974), pp.108–13; Glees, *Re-inventing Germany*, pp.58–63.
20. Morgan, *The United States and West Germany*, pp.16–17.
21. Annan, *Changing Enemies*, p.215.
22. See John Ford Gorlay, *The Founding of the Federal Republic of Germany* (Chicago, IL: Chicago University Press, 1958), ch. II, esp. pp.96–108.

Chapter 8: The European Parliament and the Idea of European Representative Government

1. Altiero Spinelli, *L'Europa non cade dal cielo* (Bologna: Il Mulino, 1960), p.15.
2. Altiero Spinelli, *Come ho tentato di diventare saggio: Io, Ulisse* (Bologna: Il Mulino, 1984), pp.307–8, translation from Richard Mayne and John Pinder, with John C. de V. Roberts, *Federal Union: The Pioneers* (Basingstoke: Macmillan, 1990), p.84.
3. See Walter Lipgens, *A History of European Integration, 1945–1947* (Oxford: Clarendon Press, 1982), p.612.
4. See Mayne and Pinder, *Federal Union*, p.100.
5. Altiero Spinelli, 'Il Documento di Lavoro di Jean Monnet', in *L'Europa non cade* p.76, (reprint of an article written in July 1950).
6. *Resolutions of the Congress of Europe, The Hague, May 1948* (Brussels: The European Movement, May 1988), p.42.
7. Martin Posselt, 'The European Parliamentary Union: 1946 to 1952', in Andrea Bosco (ed.), *The Federal Idea, vol. 2* (London: Lothian Foundation Press, 1992), p.187.
8. Etienne Hirsch, *Ainsi va la vie* (Lausanne: Fondation Jean Monnet pour l'Europe, 1988), p.107.
9. Jean Monnet, *Les Etats-Unis d'Europe ont commencé: la Communauté de Charbon et de l'Acier – discours et allocutions* (Paris: Robert Laffont, 1955), pp.57–8.
10. Debates of the Common Assembly, September 1952, p.21 (author's translation).
11. Hendrik Brugmans, in *Le Parlement européen: pouvoirs, élection, rôle, futur*, Colloque of the Institut d'Etudes Techniques Européennes (IEJE), University of Liège, 1976, p.287 (author's translation).
12. Ibid., p.167 (author's translation).
13. Georges Vedel, 'Mythes de l'Europe et Europe des Mythes', *Revue du Marché Commun,* October 1967 (author's translation).
14. The development of the role of MEPs, together with other aspects of the European Parliament's development, is analysed in Richard Corbett, *The European Parliament's Role in European Union Integration* (Basingstoke: Macmillan, 1998).
15. See Commission of the European Communities, 'The Budget: Facts and Figures', in SEC(93), (Brussels: Commission, 1993), p.13.
16. Miriam Camps, *European Unification in the Sixties: From the Veto to the Crisis* (New York: McGraw-Hill, 1966), p.59.
17. *Debates of the European Parliament,* 24 May 1984.
18. Report of the Ad Hoc Committee on Institutional Affairs ('Dooge Committee'), *Bulletin of the European Communities* 3-1985, p.102.
19. EP document A2-0332/88, 'Report drawn up on behalf of the Committee for Institutional Affairs on the strategy of the European Parliament for achieving European Union' (rapporteur Mr F. Herman), voted on 16 February 1989, *Official Journal of the European Communities* 69, 20 March 1989, p.145.
20. EP Minutes, 11 July 1990, *Official Journal of the European Communities* 23, 17 February 1990, p.97.

21. EP Minutes, 10 February 1994, *Official Journal of the European Communities* 61, 28 February 1994, p.155.

Chapter 9: Foundations for Democracy in the European Union

1. Robert A. Dahl, *Democracy and its Critics* (New Haven, CT: Yale University Press, 1989), pp.2, 18–20, 316–20; David Held, *Democracy and the Global Order: From the Modern State to Cosmopolitan Governance* (Cambridge: Polity Press, 1995), pp.32, 73, 143, 227.
2. Dahl, *Democracy*, p.31.
3. E.H. Kossmann, 'Freedom in seventeenth-century Dutch thought and practice', in Jonathan I. Israel (ed.), *The Anglo-Dutch Moment: Essays on the Glorious Revolution and its World Impact* (Cambridge: Cambridge University Press, 1991), pp.291–2.
4. Jonathan I. Israel, 'The Dutch role in the Glorious Revolution', in Israel, *The Anglo-Dutch Moment*, pp.120–3; and 'General Introduction', in Israel, ibid., pp.17–19.
5. Israel, 'The Dutch Role', p.161.
6. Hans Daalder, *Ancient and Modern Pluralism in the Netherlands*, The 1989 Erasmus Lectures at Harvard University (Cambridge, MA: Harvard University Press, 1989–90), pp.13–14.
7. Dahl, *Democracy*, pp.2, 30, 317–18.
8. Israel, 'General Introduction', p.30.
9. Israel, Ibid., p.38.
10. Israel, Ibid., p.25.
11. See, for example, John Keane, *Tom Paine: A Political Life* (London: Bloomsbury, 1995), pp.108–29, 304–44 and ch. 10.
12. Cited, in notes from Lord Acton's unpublished manuscripts, in G.E. Fasnacht, *Acton's Political Philosophy* (London: Hollis and Carter, 1952), p.243.
13. Dahl, *Democracy*, pp.2, 319.
14. David Held, *Models of Democracy* (Cambridge: Polity Press, 1987), pp.254–99; citation from p.299.
15. See Laski's letter of 2 November 1919 to Bertrand Russell, in Russell, *The Autobiography of Bertrand Russell 1914–1944*, vol. 2 (London: George Allen and Unwin, 1968), p.113, in which he wrote that Proudhon's *Du Principe fédératif* and *De la Justice dans la Révolution* were 'two very great books'.
16. Held, *Models of Democracy*, pp.72ff, 200, 282–99. Held cites in particular the works of C.B. Macpherson, Carole Pateman and Nicos Poulantzas.
17. Dahl, *Democracy*, p.2.
18. Held, *Democracy and the Global Order*, p.97.
19. Declaration by Robert Schuman, French Foreign Minister, 9 May 1950.
20. Jean Monnet, 'Discours au Séance d'Inauguration de la Haute Autorité', in Monnet, *les Etats-Unis d'Europe ont commencé: la Communauté Européenne de Charbon et de l'Acier – discours et allocutions* (Paris: Robert Laffont, 1955), pp.56–8.
21. Louis Joxe, *Victoires sur la nuit: Mémoires 1940–1946* (Paris: Flammarion, 1981), cited in Henri Rieben, *Des Guerres Européennes à l'Union de l'Europe*

(Lausanne: Fondation Jean Monnet pour l'Europe, 1987), pp.352–3; and personal information.

22. Altiero Spinelli, *Diario Europeo 1948/49*, a cura di Edmondo Paolini (Bologna: Il Mulino, 1989), p.142.
23. See Chapter 8, this volume.
24. See Sergio Pistone, 'Il ruolo di Altiero Spinelli nella genesi dell'art.38 della Comunità Europea di Difesa e del progetto di Comunità Politica Europea', in Gilbert Trausch (ed.), *The European Integration from the Schuman Plan to the Treaties of Rome* (Baden-Baden and Brussels: Nomos Verlag and Bruylant, 1993).
25. Article 31 ECSC; Article 164 EEC.
26. T.C. Hartley, *The Foundations of Community Law* (Oxford: Clarendon Press, 1994, 1st edition, 1981), p.55.
27. See Dahl, *Democracy*, p.320.
28. Jean-Victor Louis, 'La constitution de l'Union européenne', in Mario Telò (ed.), *Démocratie et Constitution Européenne* (Brussels: Editions de l'Université de Bruxelles, 1995), pp.332–3.
29. This is suggested in Dahl, *Democracy*, pp.338–9 and Held, *Democracy and the Global Order*, p.280.
30. Held, *Models*, p.289.
31. Held, *Democracy*, pp.22–3.
32. For a review of those policies, see John Pinder, 'The European Community and Democracy in Eastern Europe', in Geoffrey Pridham, Eric Herring and George Sanford (eds), *Building Democracy? – The International Dimension of Democratisation in Eastern Europe* (London: Cassel, 2nd edition, 1997; 1st edition London: Leicester University Press, 1994); and Pinder, 'Community against Conflict: The European Community's Contribution to Ethno-National Peace in Europe', in Abram Chayes and Antonia Chayes (eds), *Preventing Conflict in the Post-Communist World: Mobilizing International and Regional Organizations* (Washington, DC: The Brookings Institution, 1996).
33. Literature on this subject is reviewed and references are given in Eric Herring, 'International security and democratisation in Eastern Europe', in Pridham et al., *Building Democracy?*

Index

Abjuration, Act of (1581), 22–3, 108, 129n
absolutism, 1, 33–4; divine right, 33; in
    Italian city-states, 16–17; oligarchic,
    30; and property, 62; rejected by
    Dutch Republic, 1, 22, 109, 111; of
    Spain in Netherlands, 13, 14, *see also*
    monarchy
accession treaties, to EC, 99, 102
accountability, 3; in EU, 93, 100, 124
Acton, Lord, 114
Adams, John, 42, 46, 47, 49
Adenauer, Konrad, 78–9, 84, 85, 89, 117;
    and European parliamentary
    Assembly, 90, 91
Agnelli, Susanna, MEP, 96
Albu, Austin, MP, 80
America *see* United States of America
American War of Independence, 13, 56
Amsterdam Treaty (1997), 104, 105, 121,
    123
anarchy, Proudhon's use of word, 63, 64
Annan, Noel, 72, 80
Antwerp, fall of (1585), 13
arbitration, in mediaeval Flanders, 9
Aristotle, 44
armed forces, and state sovereignty, 54, 125
Arndt, Rudy, MEP, 96
Aron, Robert, 68
Artevelde, James van, 6
assemblies, popular, 6, 107
assent procedure, European Parliament, 99,
    102, 105
association agreements, with EU, 99
Athens, city-state, 1, 44, 112
Attlee, Clement, 73
Australasia, 119
Austria, 99, 102, 118–19
autocracy: in Italian city-states, 16–17;
    revolutions against, 13–14
autonomy: democratic, 115, 125–6; local,
    116; of nation-states, 3, 31; and
    nationality, 66; organisational, 1, 2,
    63–4, 66–7, 115–16, *see also*
    provincial autonomy; sovereignty

Bacon, Francis, 43
Bagehot, Walter, 56
balance of power, William III's policy, x, xi
Baldwin IX, 15
Balfe, Richard, MEP, 96

Bangemann, Martin, MEP, 96
Bank of England, 111
Batavian Republic (1798-1813), 19–20
Bavaria, political parties, 79
Belgium, 7; and Europe, 97, 100, 106, 122
Berlin, blockade and airlift, 76–7, 117
Beveridge, Sir William, 83, 87
Bevin, Ernest, 80, 81
Bill of Rights (1689), x, 38, 52, 111, 112
Bill of Rights, American, 52, 58
Bismarck, Otto von, 116
Blackstone, Sir William: on British
    Constitution, 43–4, 113; theory of
    sovereignty, 45–6, 51, 56
Blair, Tony, UK Prime Minister, 104
Bland, Richard, 47
Böckler, Hans, 82
borough charters, 5
bourgeoisie, in France, 60, 61
Bourlanges, Jean-Louis, MEP, 103
Brabant, 7, 12, 129n
Bracton, Henry de, 51
Brandt, Willy, MEP, 96
Brissot, Jacques-Pierre, Girondin leader, 60
British Constitution, 1, 7, 43–4; checks and
    balances, 36, 43–4; codification of,
    55–6; compared with American, 55–7;
    and myth of anglo-saxon purity, 45, 49
Brok, Elmar, MEP, 103
Bruges, 6, 11–12, 129n
Brugmans, Hendrik, 91
Brussels Treaty (1948), 84
budget *see* parliamentary control of budget
Buffon, Comte de, 42
Burgh, James, *Political Disquisitions*, 46
burghers: Dutch Republic, 109, 130n, *see
    also* regents
Burgundian Netherlands: as federal
    monarchy, 7–8, 16, 130n, 132n;
    provincial autonomy, 11, 16; self
    government in, 107–8
Burgundy, House of, and unification of Low
    Countries, 6, 7–8
Burke, Edmund, 43

Cahiers des doléances (1789), 60
Calvin, John, 42
Canada, 119
Canute IV, King of Denmark, 4
capitalism, and democracy, 79

Index compiled by Auriol Griffith-Jones